Raising Virginia

Raising Virginia

A Message of Hope

MaryAnn Bradley

ISBN 13: 978-1-7322171-6-4

Table of Contents

About MaryAnn Bradley

My name is MaryAnn Bradley. I grew up in the small town of Nephi, Utah. I am a mother and grandmother. I have been a homemaker my entire adult life, and I live with my husband and youngest son in House Spirngs, Missouri. I enjoy teaching life skills and gospel topics. I have taught all age groups within my church family.

Parenting children is a lifelong venture. It can be challenging and rewarding in every aspect. "Raising Virginia" is about my weaknesses as a young mother and how I dealt with them. It is also a story of hope for those parents who have children who have been placed on selective serotonin reuptake inhibitors (SSRIs) and would like to find alternative options to those medications.

This story tells how, over the years, as Virginia grew physically and emotionally, we struggled with disciplining her the best way for her personality. Virginia was an intense, strong-willed child. Many times during her younger years,

I lost my temper and was physically harsh with her. She is very forgiving and forgave me for those mistakes.

Virginia was placed on anti-anxiety, then anti-depressant meds at eight years old. This is the story of how those medications affected her, and how we eventually weaned her off the medications on our own. It was harder than I imagined it would be.

Virginia has become an amazing, vibrant, and bold woman. She is not afraid to speak her mind. It has taken faith in God and many prayers on all our parts to get her to where she is today.

Introduction
Why I Chose to Write this Story

Why did I choose to write "Raising Virginia?" Several times during Virginia's teenage years, I thought about writing what it was like raising her, including all my personal and our family struggles. I wanted to help other parents, who had children with high intensity and other characteristics, know they are not alone.

I didn't think I was ready to tell my story while Virginia was still in high school. However, one year after she graduated from high school and started attending college, I received the conviction that it was time to begin. It would be several months before I actually moved forward with that decision.

It all started when I was entering into a sacred building that belonged to our church. A friend of mine was entering the building at the same time. I knew her from a previous congregation I had attended in Jefferson City, Missouri. I had an impression to talk with her and discuss my idea to write a story about raising Virginia.

Before I spoke with my friend, I had not thought of writing a book with someone else. I knew she had experienced more severe trials of child rearing than I could ever imagine. For this reason, I did not want to approach her. I shrugged off the impression and entered the building. At the end of my visit, but while still in the building, I entered into the women's restroom. I saw this friend of mine again. Once again, I received the impression to talk to her about writing Virginia's story.

I noticed she was teary-eyed so I was a little apprehensive to broach the subject. I persevered and walked up to her and gave her a hug. Then I proceeded to tell her my thoughts on writing a story about raising Virginia and gave her a brief synopsis. She told me she, too, had recently been thinking about writing a story about her own child-rearing experiences. We discussed the fact that both our children had been placed on selective serotonin reuptake inhibitors (SSRIs) and that these drugs had negatively affected them.

That night, when I returned home, I told Virginia about my experience that day. I spoke to her about my plans to write a book about raising her and asked her how she felt about it. She said she thought it was a good idea, but didn't say much more than that.

Less than two months later, the night before Virginia entered the Missionary Training Center to serve an eighteen-month proselyting mission for our church, we visited with some family members. We discussed with them their experiences with SSRIs and how these drugs had affected them and their families. The discussion led to many tears. We had a heart-touching interaction for more than two hours.

That night, as Virginia and I prepared to go to bed, she looked me in the eye and said, "Mom, you have to write your story!" I believe until participating in the evening's conversation, she only half-heartedly agreed that I should undertake this project. After all, this story would be mostly about her and how we struggled to raise her because of our lack of understanding. After Virginia witnessed that others, including ones in our own extended family, were experiencing great trials because of intense emotional behaviors and the effects SSRIs had on them, she was completely on board with me writing this story. And so the journey of this book began.

Chapter One
Birth to Five Years Old

Virginia Joyce Bradley was born in 1997 to Mark and MaryAnn Bradley. We were thrilled to have a new baby girl. She was adorable and perfect. When Mark and I knew we were expecting our fourth child, I told him it was his turn to pick a name. I had chosen the names for the first three children and he had agreed. Mark chose the name for our fourth child, which we knew would be a girl, but he wouldn't tell me what it was for several months. He wanted to wait until she was born to tell me! I finally convinced him to share the name he had chosen. She was named after both her grandmothers. Mark named her in honor of his mother, Virginia Villalobos, also known as Grandma Ginny, and my mother, Joyce Bracken.

Virginia was born in Ogden, Utah. My labor, delivery, and recovery with her were the best out of all five of our children. I didn't have an epidural, and she was born after twelve hours of labor and delivery combined.

When I brought Virginia home from the hospital, her older siblings fawned over her and she was not left alone very often. I remember that on her blessing day we laid her down on the bed next to her cousin, who was two weeks younger, and took pictures. Virginia's face was beet red because she screamed the whole time.

During my pregnancy with Virginia, I experienced some unusual highs and lows of emotion. At the time, I didn't feel like I was any more emotional during my pregnancy with her but I did have some days that stood out in my mind when I seemed very out of sorts. One of those times happened one morning when I was trying to fix my oldest son John-Michael's bunk bed. I was feeling so frustrated that I went and grabbed the hammer and I started banging away on the metal frame, crying and yelling as I did. Then, not wanting my older two children to continue to see my crazy emotions, I went into the garage and yelled and cried some more. Amazingly, unbeknownst to me, my husband felt as if he should turn around and come back home. He had already started driving to work that morning, but received the impression to come back. He arrived home in time to find me sobbing. He just held me and talked to me until I calmed down and gathered myself. I am sure he was bewildered by my behavior, and I would have been perplexed as well if I were him. To this day, I do not remember what caused that particular crazy outburst, but I'm sure it had to do with the hormone levels in my body. Years later, I sometimes wondered if those emotions may have contributed to the intense child Virginia was and is. The more I learn about myself and the health and development of unborn babies, I believe my emotions played a part in Virginia's emotional development while in utero. One of my older sisters who is a nurse has discussed this type of phenomena with me. I decided to do a little research concerning ties between a mother's mental health and its effects on the fetus. These next several paragraphs show information I chose to add. I found multiple articles of interest, including this one about a mother's mental state and how it influences the baby while in the womb.

Change in Mother's Mental State Can Influence Her Baby's Development Before and After Birth

As a fetus grows, it's constantly getting messages from its mother. It's not just hearing her heartbeat and whatever music she might play to her belly; it also gets chemical signals through the placenta. A new study, which will be published in Psychological Science, a journal of the Association for Psychological Science, finds that this includes signals about the mother's mental state. If the mother is depressed, that affects how the baby develops after it's born.

Curt A. Sandman, Elysia P. Davis, and Laura M. Glynn of the University of California-Irvine study how the mother's psychological state affects a developing fetus. For this study, they recruited pregnant women and checked them for depression before and after they gave birth. They also gave their babies tests after they were born to see how well they were developing.

They found something interesting: what mattered to the babies was if the environment was consistent before and after birth. That is, the babies who did best were those who either had mothers who were healthy both before and after birth, and those whose mothers were depressed before birth and stayed depressed afterward. What slowed the babies' development was changing conditions—a mother who went from depressed before birth to healthy after or healthy before birth to depressed after. "We must admit, the strength of this finding surprised us," Sandman says.

Now, the cynical interpretation of our results would be that if a mother is depressed before birth, you should leave her that way for the well-being of the infant. "A more reasonable approach would be, to treat women who present with prenatal depression. Sandman says. "We know how to deal with depression." The problem is, women are rarely screened for depression before birth.

In the long term, having a depressed mother could lead

to neurological problems and psychiatric disorders, Sandman says. In another study, his team found that older children whose mothers were anxious during pregnancy, which often is co-morbid with depression, have differences in certain brain structures. It will take studies lasting decades to figure out exactly what having a depressed mother means to a child's long-term health.

"We believe that the human fetus is an active participant in its own development and is collecting information for life after birth," Sandman says. "It's preparing for life based on messages the mom is providing."

For a copy of the research article and access to other Psychological Science research findings, please contact: Anna Mikulak, Association for Psychological Science, 202.293.9300, <u>amikulak@psychological-science.org.</u>

I found this previous article very enlightening, especially the statement "A baby is preparing for life based on the information the mother is providing."

I'm sure Virginia developed some of her characteristics and attributes according to the information she received while in utero. I also believe children already have a basic set of God-given characteristics they are born with. Then they can develop other personality traits while in the womb.

17

I believe that, at times during my pregnancy with Virginia, I may have suffered short bouts of depression or other types of emotional distress or anxiety. I acknowledge the fact that many women suffer intense emotions throughout pregnancy. During my pregnancy with Virginia, I was more emotional than during any of my other pregnancies. I also thought about the following—that the effects on the mother's emotions might also be affected by the emotions of the unborn baby. Could it be that I was experiencing emotions Virginia was feeling while in utero? Possibly. I tend to believe that the emotions of mother and fetus are interchangeable, i.e., their emotions could be felt both ways.

I want to share another article I found in my research to begin to substantiate my belief about a mother feeling the emotions of her unborn baby. Again, this is my own hypothesis. Before quoting the article, I would like to quote a verse from the King James version of the Christian Bible in the Book of Jeremiah. This is why I believe Virginia already had much of her characteristics before she was born. I quote this scripture to verify my thoughts on this.

Jeremiah 1:4-5: "Then the word of the Lord came unto me, saying, Before I formed thee in the belly I knew thee; and before thou camest forth out of the womb I sanctified thee...."

Here is the excerpt from the article:

There is a growing body of research showing that babies in the womb feel, taste, learn, and have some level of consciousness. One study had babies in the womb receiving "vibroacoustic stimulation" (Gonzalez-Gonzalez et al., 2006). That is a fancy way of saying sound waves were transmitted. For comparison purposes, there was also a control group that did not receive the treatment. After they were born, the babies who had received the stimulation were again given the same treatment. The result was that these babies recognized the signal and tended to calm down after receiving the signal. The researchers concluded that fetal life is able to learn and memorize with this capacity lasting into neonatal life (post-birth).

In other research, Anthony DeCasper and William Fifer created a nipple that was connected to an audio device (Kolata, 1984). This nipple test was given to 10 newborn babies. If a child sucked in one way they would hear their mother's voice. Sucking in a different pattern would cause the child to hear another woman's voice. The researchers found that the babies sucked in a way to hear their mothers. The same experiment was done using the sound of the mother's heartbeat and that of a male voice. The result was that the babies sucked in such a way as to hear the mother's heart beat more often than the male voice.

DeCasper later did another test where he had sixteen pregnant women read a children's book. They read the book out loud twice a day for the last 6.5 weeks of their pregnancy. Once born, the babies were given the nipple test previously mentioned where they could listen either to their mother reading the original children's book that was used or another book. The babies sucked to hear the original children's book. What DeCasper concluded was that a prenatal auditory experience can influence auditory preferences after birth.

Gonzalez-Gonzalez, N. L., Suarez, M. N., Perez-Pinero, B., Armas, H., Domenech, E., & Bartha, J. L. (2006). Persistence of fetal memory into neonatal life. Acta Obstetricia et Gynecologica, 85, 1160-1164. doi:10.1080/00016340600855854

Kolata, Gina (1984). <u>Studying learning in the womb</u>. Science, 225, 302-303. doi:10.1126/science.6740312

Web url address is: <u>https://psychcentral.com/blog/emotional-trauma-in-the-womb/</u>

Thus, if a child after it is born seeks out the familiar sounds that brought them comfort while in the womb, why not conclude that the mother could feel the emotions of the baby through her own psychological system, while she is carrying him or her? So my hypothesis is that mothers share emotions back and forth while they are carrying their unborn babies. So I believe it is possible I felt Virginia's emotions while in utero.

After Virginia was born, I had one day of postpartum sadness or depression but nothing very serious. I had experienced this same phenomena with each of my other children after their births as well. I do not have evidence that my emotional state had an effect on the development of Virginia's intense personality, but just as music, reading aloud and other things a mother does or experiences while she is pregnant affect an unborn child, I believe these findings about the emotional health of mothers playing a part on how their babies develop related to what took place during my pregnancy with Virginia. It makes sense to me that my emotional state during my pregnancy would have an effect on how my children developed both in and outside of the womb; particularly I recognized this in Virginia because of her intense or high sensory personality.

Virginia grew and progressed quickly through each stage from infant to toddler. She learned to walk at eight months old and talked around the same time as well. Most children do not learn to walk that early. She walked and talked earlier than any of our other children by at least two and a half months. John-Michael is the only other child that walked before he was a year old. He was eleven months old when he began walking. As Virginia grew, she seemed to be easily comforted if she could suck on a pacifier. We kept one on hand in every bag because they were so easily misplaced.

She was so full of energy and smiles. Nearly all of her

baby pictures show a smiling, happy, vibrant little girl, except for the one picture on the day of her blessing. One afternoon, when Virginia was less than eighteen months old and while we were living in Roy, Utah, she had a minor tantrum. Mark made a particular comment on how awful she was. I was aghast by his comment because I was an overprotective mother. I asked him not to ever say anything like that again. I acknowledged that her behavior was un-acceptable. I remembered learning years earlier that when we say something out loud about a person in their presence, it can affect the way they feel and think about themselves. Mark was good to remember this and never repeated his statement.

Mark never spent a lot of time around younger children while he was growing up and especially not around a child with such intense behavior as Virginia exhibited. He spent time with his uncle and aunt, who had fourteen children, and they were a very talkative and rambunctious family. He was not around them on a daily basis, which led to my assumption that he might not handle a child's intense be-havior very well. Nonetheless, Mark handled our children's crying and tantrums quite well.

In my youth, I spent many hours babysitting all types of personalities. I got frustrated with little ones who screamed because I didn't know how to comfort them. Because of this, I was a little nervous about having children who might cry a lot. One day after our first daughter was born, I had an instance when I felt a welling up of emotion because of her constant crying. These feelings only lasted momentarily. I never felt frustrated with my children's tears when they were babies because I loved them so much. I didn't feel that there was a problem with Virginia's behavior at all in the beginning. She didn't seem to cry any more than her older siblings had in those early months. From the onset, we never thought of Virginia as any different than our other children. Raising her became challenging, though.

Virginia was easy to put in bed at night as long as she had her pacifier and could reach her belly button. She had to have her index finger in her belly button and her pacifier in her mouth so she could fall asleep. Before I realized that she had this fascination or tactical sensory need to touch her belly button, I put a pair of pajamas on her that zipped up the front. The first night I put her to bed with this type of pajamas on and laid her down, she immediately reached for her belly button. Since she was unable to reach her bellybutton, she cried and fussed intensely while pulling at her pajamas. As soon as I unzipped her pajamas, she stuck her finger in her belly button and sucked contently on her pacifier. From that day on, during her first year, I always made sure she could access her tummy when I laid her down in bed.

She slept in a crib until she was about a year old. Her crib was in her brother John-Michael's room. When she woke up during the night and cried, all I needed to do was put her pacifier back in her mouth and she would settle right back down again. One night John-Michael asked if he could come and sleep with us if she cried. I agreed. I later found out that once or twice he pulled her pacifier out on purpose so he could come sleep with mom and dad. I can't say I blamed him, though; I would have done the same thing.

While Virginia was still a baby and into her toddler years, her older siblings loved to play with her all her waking hours. She was well loved by all of us. She had beautiful olive skin and dark chocolate brown eyes. Her smile was and still is contagious. She has a smile that could light up a room and your heart. She had a very loud and infectious laugh and still does. As she grew older into her teen years, I could always find her in a large crowd of people if I listened long enough because of her distinct loud laugh.

When she was a little over a year old, I discovered that she started screaming if someone didn't give her what she wanted right away. I didn't recognize this as manipulation at the time; I just thought she was a very insistent toddler. At seventeen months, she tried to pull a lamp off an end table while screaming for something she wanted. I was unable to calm her down so I put her in her crib and left her in her room. After she'd been screaming for ten minutes, I went into her room and asked if she was ready to get out of her crib. She screamed at the top of her lungs, "No!" She remained there for another ten to fifteen minutes. When she finally calmed down, I quietly opened the bedroom door and asked if she was ready to get out and be happy. She said

"Yes!" with exuberance, and was content and sweet again. She played happily the rest of the evening with her older siblings Janessa and John-Michael.

The next morning, when I removed her pajamas, I noticed that both of her knees were black and blue. I came to the conclusion that she must have banged her knees repeatedly against the slats on the crib while she was screaming the night before. I hadn't personally ever experienced such intensity in a child before, and this was just the beginning.

At eighteen months came the beginning of ten years of tantrums that ranged from one a day to five or six per day. The tantrums would last anywhere from five minutes to forty-five minutes; usually it was the latter. In between her tantrums, she was full of energy and joy.

Virginia loved playing outside. The outdoors seemed to keep her the most satisfied and content. She would play for hours and hours outside if she was allowed. I have a friend with an eighteen-year-old autistic daughter who loves to be outside for hours. In fact, my friend usually cannot get her daughter to come in when it is warm outside. This young adult sometimes stays outside until long after midnight.

Virginia also developed a deep love for animals. From the time she was a toddler to today, she adored animals. We had a cat named Mckay when Virginia was born. Mckay was a well-loved family pet and he lived with us for seventeen years. He came with us when we moved to Missouri from Utah. We relocated to West Plains in southern Missouri and bought a home out in the country. This made it possible for us to have several animals over the years. Along with the home we bought, we inherited some wild cats that all lived outside. Eventually the wildcats ran away. We adopted several cats and dogs over the five years we lived there.

All our animals lived outdoors except for our black-and-white cat, Mckay. In later years, I succumbed to pressure and we ended up with two indoor dogs. These animals occupied Virginia's attention, brought her happiness, and gave her an outlet for some of her intensity.

As she grew older, she often monopolized a particular pet's attention all to herself. The name of this particular pet was Christmas. He was a very small Pomeranian. She didn't want anyone else to hold him when she had his attention. She would not let the dog run to her younger brother even if he (Christmas) wanted to. She would purposefully encourage the dog to growl and bark at her younger brother Wesley whenever he walked past her.

In the early years of Virginia's life when she had tantrums, I just wrote it off as the terrible twos, then the horrible threes. I didn't realize that her behavior wasn't the normal terrible-two variety.

One of her first memorable tantrums away from home happened while we were out shopping. We lived in Roy, Utah at the time. I did most of my shopping at the Hill Air Force Base Commissary. Virginia was approximately two years old on this particular grocery shopping outing. As I shopped that afternoon, Virginia asked for something in the store. I said, "no." She threw herself on the floor, kicking and screaming. I was self-conscious about her behavior and felt as if all the other shoppers' eyes were riveted on me. I couldn't get out of that grocery store fast enough!

Virginia screamed the entire time through the checkout and halfway home, which was about a twenty-minute drive. She shrieked for about forty-five minutes. I tried several times to talk to her kindly and patiently but to no avail. She didn't get what she wanted and she wasn't about to let up on her screaming. As we drove home, she continued yelling.

Finally, I lost my temper and angrily snapped at her. When I couldn't take any more, I pulled over to the side of the freeway and stopped the car. More squalling ensued. She demanded that we go back to get what she wanted. I turned around in my seat and flicked her lip, scolding her loudly for her outburst. I was not calm.

When I turned back to the steering wheel, I was horrified to see a police officer at my car window! He thought I was in need of assistance and had stopped to help. Needless to say, I was completely embarrassed because I had let a small child get the best of my emotions once again.

After Virginia grew into her fourth year, the tantrums not only continued; they increased in intensity. At this point, she would usually have anywhere from two to six tantrums in one day. Virginia was a daddy's girl and she loved to spend time with her dad. I have a picture of her when she was two years old sitting on the couch next to her daddy wearing only a diaper and a ball cap. She would sit next to him and watch football.

Virginia has always remained closely attached emotionally to her father and I always appreciated that. Mark was usually home every evening in the first three years of her young life. Virginia didn't seem to have quite as many tantrums when daddy was around because she couldn't manipulate him as easily as she could me. The only individuals in our family she wasn't able to manipulate while she was young were Janessa and Mark.

She manipulated Wesley when they were young. He would ask if he could play with Virginia and her friends when they came over. She would let Wesley play only if he would pretend to be the dog and stay in the corner. When Wesley became a teenager, she was unable to manipulate him anymore. In spite of her manipulation of Wesley, she adored him.

When Wesley was born, Virginia was almost three-and-a-half years old. Three days after I came home from the hospital with Wesley, I was in my bathroom, and Virginia came looking for me. She marched proudly into my bathroom carrying her new baby brother upside down by one leg! I amazingly kept my composure, which was unusual for me in that type of situation. I gently took Wesley from her. I knew she might drop him if I panicked or raised my voice. I cradled Wesley in my arms and thanked Virginia for bringing him to me. I later explained to her that she was never to get him out of the crib again so he wouldn't get hurt.

Virginia wanted to spend as much time as possible with her new baby brother. She shared her room with him while he was still a baby because we had a small home. With Wesley as the newest addition to our family, Virginia didn't receive as much of my attention as she had before. She wanted to stay nearby as I nursed him during the day. She had a few more tantrums to vie for my attention, but I didn't notice the increase in number. As she grew, she usually didn't throw tantrums in public like the one at the grocery store. It seemed that the majority of her outbursts happened at home. This and the fact that most of her tantrums occurred while Mark was at work helped our counselor, years later, to pin down one of her behavior problems as manipulation.

Before I discovered she was manipulating me, I began to believe that Virginia was just a rebellious child because her outbursts were usually at home. When we met our counselor, Mrs. Jones, when Virginia was eight, I was ignorant of the fact that a youngster could be manipulative. I was also still learning about "The Spirited Child," a book I discovered through our first counselor in West Plains. I didn't know much about spirited children at that time.

In Virginia's fifth year of life, we were walking home from a friend's house. They lived one-and-a-half miles away from us down a dirt road. We were living out in the country in southern Missouri at this time. I was pushing Virginia and her baby brother in our double stroller with our two older children walking alongside.

Virginia started to scream at me that she wanted to go back to our friend's home. I calmly reminded her it was time to go home and put Wesley down in bed for a nap. She kicked and screamed for me to turn around. No amount of reasoning would calm her. She continued yelling about how I didn't know what I was doing and berating me, which usually got under my skin. I am sure she subconsciously knew her screaming caused me to feel frustrated. Eventually I lost my composure. I reached around the stroller and smacked her mouth because her badgering, belittling and screaming had increased. I missed her mouth and got her nose, which began to bleed.

At that moment, I felt like the worst mother in the world! A car passed by us right as her nose began bleeding and later came back with a wet wash cloth. I was sure the person in the car saw the whole ordeal and I thought he would report me to DFS (Department of Family Services). I was physically sick the rest of the day. I was afraid Virginia and/or all of my children would be taken from us. I knew I needed help with her but at the time I didn't know where to turn. I believed the problem was all mine and that it had to do with my lack of patience. I believed I just needed to learn how to handle the situations patiently, which to some degree was true. I truly believe that, if we had learned early on how to parent her effectively, her behavior problems would not have increased as much or she may not have had any at all. Hindsight is always twenty/twenty, of course, but I thought that with the proper diet and counseling we would have had a much smoother ride.

Virginia's daily tantrums ranged from whining and crying to stomping on top of her own feet. She would scream and kick the walls, along with other unacceptable behaviors. At this point in her life, she didn't lash out at people to harm them. She only harmed herself, which consisted of the toe crunching and stomping on her own feet.

Often during her fourth and fifth year, if she threw a tantrum, I would put her in her room. She wouldn't stay in her room unless I held the door closed. My husband and I decided to turn the lock around on the door so I could lock it from the outside. After we changed the lock, she would lie on her bed and kick the walls or door, and sometimes the pictures on the other side of the wall would nearly fall off.

Another thing I noticed about her was that she was overly sensitive to tags in her clothing or wrinkles in her socks. Anything that would normally cause a child to ask for help to smooth things out caused her to cry and fuss incessantly. Another problem she experienced was she got car sick easily. I researched a little bit about sensory processing issues and there are several correlations with this particular disorder that seemed to fit Virginia's patterns as a toddler. She did not have the extremes that children with

Sensory Processing Disorder have, but she displayed a few issues that matched up with children who have Sensory Processing Sensitivity. (I've added some information below that I looked up about this particular sensitivity, which pegs Virginia precisely.)

Sensory processing sensitivity (SPS), a personality trait, a high measure of which defines a highly sensitive person (HSP), has been described as having hypersensitivity to external stimuli, a greater depth of cognitive processing, and high emotional reactivity. The terms SPS and HSP were coined in the mid-1990s by psychologists Elaine Aron and husband Arthur Aron, with SPS being measured by <u>Aron's Highly Sensitive Person Scale (HSPS)</u> *questionnaire. Other researchers have applied various other terms to denote this responsiveness to stimuli that is evidenced in humans and other species.*

According to the Arons and colleagues, people with high SPS comprise about 15-20% of the population and are thought to process sensory data more deeply due to the nature of their central nervous system. Although many researchers consistently related high SPS to negative outcomes, Aron and colleagues state that high SPS is a personality trait and not a disorder; other researchers have associated it with increased responsiveness to both positive and negative influences.

Elaine Aron's 1996 book, The Highly Sensitive Person, defined a population of people having "increased sensitivity to stimulation" and who "are more aware of subtleties and process information in a deeper, more reflective way." In 1997 Elaine and Arthur Aron formally identified sensory processing sensitivity (SPS), the scientific term for highly sensitive or hypersensitivity, as the defining trait of highly sensitive persons (HSPs). By way of definition, Aron & Aron (1997) wrote that sensory processing here refers not to the sense organs as such, but to what occurs as sensory information is transmitted to or processed in the brain. The trait has been described as "neither flaw nor gift... an amplifier of an environment's effects."

Aron's professional journal articles and self-help publications have focused on distinguishing high SPS from socially reticent behavior and disorders with which high SPS can be confused; overcoming the social unacceptability that can cause low self-esteem; and emphasizing the advantages of high SPS to balance the disadvantages emphasized by others.

In 2015 Elizabeth Bernstein wrote in the Wall Street Journal that HSPs were "having a moment," noting that several hundred research studies had been conducted on topics related to HSPs' high sensitivity, and that a First International Scientific Conference on

High Sensitivity or Sensory Processing Sensitivity had been held at the Vrije Universiteit Brussel. By 2015, more than a million copies of The Highly Sensitive Person had been sold. https://en.wikipedia.org/wiki/ Sensory_processing_sensitivity

I noticed in this article that Virginia matched up with the description of a highly sensitive person. I recommend reading the whole article to find out if your child is a highly sensitive person or if he or she actually has Sensory Processing Disorder. Raising children is a journey of a lifetime; we all make mistakes along the way and learn new things that we can do to help our children excel with the traits they possess.

Back to Virginia's growing years and the challenges we faced. In southern Missouri, we lived out in the country and the roads usually twisted, turned and took you up and down. I didn't recognize that she was experiencing car sickness in the beginning. I didn't come to this realization about car sickness because she usually would get cranky while we were in the car if I didn't give her what she wanted when she wanted it. Over time, I eventually learned that the poor little sweetie was whining when we were driving because her tummy was upset. The other children did not seem to have a problem as severely as she did with the windy roads so this sensitivity was not immediately apparent to me.

While we were living in West Plains, and during the

first few years of homeschooling, I met with several other mothers every Friday for playtime. This group was enjoyable for the children and the adult interaction for the mothers helped encourage me through my adversities as a homeschool mom. A good friend of mine offered her home as the meeting place for this group and we would spend two or three hours together discussing homeschooling ideas and just socializing.

Our children also had the opportunity to visit and play with other children of all different ages. One particular Friday morning, as I was preparing to leave my friend's home after Friday morning mother's group, my good friend noticed that Virginia was arguing with me about something and Virginia was only four at the time. Cindy (name has been changed) said to me, "Someday that girl is going to be the CEO of some company!" I smiled wanly and tried to get Virginia to comply and go to the van. I look back now as I see the progress she has made and realize how right Cindy was.

There was a particular homeschool Christian family group camp in southern Missouri that we attended for a few years each spring while Virginia was pretty young. One morning at camp, while I was chatting with some other mothers, Virginia came to me cranky as could be. She was three at the time. I finally found the problem; one of her socks had a wrinkle in it. As soon as the wrinkle was smoothed out and she was sure it wouldn't bother her anymore, she skipped off happy and bouncy again.

I didn't understand this intense fuss about her tags and wrinkles. At this stage in Virginia's life, I still didn't realize I should ask my pediatrician, or anyone else, for help. I just thought she was tough to deal with at times and I was a bad mom for losing my cool. After the Christian camp ordeal with her wrinkled socks, I was careful to smooth out her socks before putting her shoes on. I also was sure to cut the tags off her shirts. I believe many parents beat themselves up emotionally when they experience this type of adversity with their children. We are too embarrassed to ask for help. I was too embarrassed and ashamed of my lack of self-control.

In those early years of Virginia's life, the Internet and the ease to research anything you had questions about did not exist. When she started into her tantrums, I felt she was just a rebellious child and I didn't know how to change that. I read several books about child rearing and also signed up for and took the Love and Logic course. I was constantly trying to find ways to change and improve my parenting; I wanted to be a better parent and learn how to act instead of react.

Virginia hated interruptions while she was watching television. One day I noticed that she would wiggle her bottom while watching TV. I finally discovered she needed to go to the bathroom. No amount of coaxing could get her to leave the show she was watching and go potty. She wouldn't walk away from the television and go to the bathroom even during a commercial. She argued incessantly that she didn't need to go potty and would not go until the show or video ended. I know many mothers experience this kind of frustration; it is just part of child rearing.

Even after she was potty trained, Virginia would often have accidents because she waited too long. If I turned off the television and told her to go to the bathroom, she would throw herself into a twenty- to thirty-minute tantrum. This waiting too long to urinate became a two- to three-year ordeal. During one of our family trips to South Carolina, when Virginia was about three years old, she had a Urinary Tract Infection (UTI), but I didn't know it. This occurred right before Wesley was born. I believe this was the first time she had a UTI.

On our return trip home from South Carolina, I was still ignorant of the problems she was experiencing. We stopped at a gas station to refuel and everyone had gone to the bathroom. Less than ten minutes down the road, Virginia piped up, "I have to go potty!" I was shocked that she had to go again. This happened two or three more times within an hour. I felt frustrated. I finally came to the realization that she must have a UTI. She often contracted urinary infections because she held her urine in too long; at least that is what the doctor later concluded.

There were many times while raising Virginia that I mistakenly interpreted her erratic behavior as rebellion rather than trying to see if there might be an underlying medical problem. This medical problem she developed was an added stress to what I was already experiencing with her intense behavior patterns.

I was a mother of four small children. My husband was in the Air National Guard and was activated after September 11, 2001. He left home in October of that year and was gone for nine months the first time. This event that affected the whole world affected our little family for quite some time. Mark traveled quite a bit after September 11th. I often felt very overwhelmed at times trying to hold down the fort.

Because I didn't reach out for help from friends or my church family like I should have, I loaded myself down with more stress. I didn't realize how important it was to take the time everyone needs to refuel. I felt like I needed to do it all myself and didn't want to burden anyone else with my problems or stresses. Many years later, I began to notice overworked moms who needed a break from their little ones. Looking back, I see how much more effective I could have been as a parent if I had been willing to open up and ask for help. We don't need to do everything ourselves; we need to reach out to family, friends, or health professionals to help raise children, especially challenging children.

Eventually, at around age five, Virginia developed a kidney infection because of her constant UTIs and was very ill. The night before I took her into the physician, her fever spiked to 103-104 degrees. My husband was away on a military assignment. I had no one to stay with the children so I could run to the store and buy some liquid ibuprofen. I realize now—fifteen years later—that I could have set up a support group of mothers within my church or community to reach out to when I needed help. That is something anyone can do.

We lived out in the country. I didn't have a support group and I was too shy to call someone from my church that late at night for help, especially when I lived so far out from town. The nearest store was at least fifteen to twenty minutes away by car. I tried coaxing Virginia to take an ibuprofen pill I had cut in half, but she refused. I was frustrated and worried about her. When I tried to force her to swallow it by putting it in her mouth several times, she just spit it out and cried all the more. I prayed for help. I placed cold washcloths on her head and gave her water until she cooled a little and fell asleep. Now I am thankful that she refused to swallow the ibuprofen. It may have been too much medication for her little body.

The next day at the doctor's office, she was diagnosed with a kidney infection. The physician was perplexed that she had a kidney infection at such a young age. I explained Virginia's history of urinary infections, and how she refused to go to the bathroom. He consoled me, telling me that many children go through that "not wanting to go to the bathroom" stage. He also explained that her kidney situation was not impossible, assuring me that she could easily be healed with a course of common antibiotics.

I later discovered a wonderful cranberry concentrate that worked wonders for UTIs. Even as Virginia grew into her preteen years, she was prone to infections. She usually got UTIs once a year. As long as I gave her the cranberry concentrate in a glass of water three times a day, her infection would go away within a day and a half. The liquid concentrate was a much better option than trying to encourage her to swallow pills.

She eventually grew out of the constant urinary infections, especially when she decided to go to the bathroom at the time she needed to rather than waiting. I believe she just thought life would pass her by and she would miss something so she didn't want to stop to take time to run to the bathroom. This is a common trait for those with high sensory sensitivity. This may seem silly and unnecessary information, but it was just another piece to the puzzle I was trying to put together to understand Virginia, her personality, and her characteristics.

Another public tantrum occurred at a dentist's office when she was a little over four years old. A few days before our appointment, she had fallen off our playground slide and hit the side of her head, which resulted in a very dark, purple black eye. Before we left home on the day of the appointment, she had drawn on herself with a red pen. These red pen marks looked like fingernail scratches up and down her arm. I didn't notice the pen marks on her arms until after we arrived at the dentist's office. While waiting for our turn to see the dentist, I noticed that she was wiggling in her chair so I knew she needed to go to the bathroom. The office only had one bathroom. I took her in and asked her to use the facilities. She proceeded to scream at me, "No, I don't want to go potty!", "Don't touch me, you're hurting me!" I thought the receptionist was probably thinking I was hurting her, especially considering her physical appearance upon arriving at the office.

I was overly conscious about her behavior because of past tantrums in public. My experience and knowledge of the area of Missouri we lived in led me to believe that people would call DFS for anything they deemed abuse. I worried too much about her throwing a fit in public. Nothing ever resulted from her screaming in the bathroom except my embarrassment and worry. It is a memory that stuck with me over the years. I know that if I had had the insight to get some help early on in Virginia's life, I would have learned to parent her with less frustration on my part and fewer situations of losing my temper.

We often went to Utah for a week or more during the summers. One year we traveled to Utah without Mark when Virginia was under seven years old; it was exhausting. She had tantrums every day. One day on our drive home was particularly rough. I was the only driver so we stopped often. We were driving through one of those lovely flat boring stretches of Kansas. I don't recall what set Virginia off, but she became upset about something. She began screaming and fighting with her older sister and wouldn't stop. I tried to reason with the girls and encouraged Virginia to calm down while I was driving, but to no avail. I pulled off the freeway and told them both to get out and walk. I drove fifty or sixty yards or more and then let them get back in the van. I look back now and think that experience must have been really scary for both of them. They may have thought I really might leave them there on the side of the road and not come back.

On that same trip, we stopped at a restaurant for breakfast. Before we received our meal, Virginia began arguing with me and her emotions began to escalate so I took her outside. I am sure I lost my temper and yelled at her. I usually didn't yell at her in public and she knew it. She continued to argue and yell at me. By the time she calmed down and we returned inside the restaurant, the other children were already finished eating.

Trying to encourage Virginia to calm down once she hit a certain point in her explosion cycle never worked for me. I hadn't learned at this point how to defuse her anger before she exploded. If I didn't nip it in the bud, she had to get back to a calm state on her own with passage of time. Looking back, I wonder if I had pulled over immediately and let Virginia and Janessa talk about why they were upset, the arguing probably never would have gotten to the height it did.

I often took trips without Mark because he was in the military. It was hard to travel without him. If the children argued or Virginia had a disagreement with anyone, I had to pull over and spend an hour or more resolving the situation or removing her from the car until she stopped screaming or yelling.

Another traumatic experience happened when we lived in West Plains. Virginia was between five and six years old and she was having one of her daily screaming fits because she wanted something that I said no to. She continued to kick and scream so I set her out on our deck and shut the sliding glass door. She began kicking the door with all her might and it rattled and shook. I realized my mistake and opened the door and told her not to kick the glass because it could shatter and break into hundreds of small pieces. I explained to her that she might get cut severely if she continued kicking the door.

I slid the door shut again but she continued to kick the door and scream. I gave up on leaving her out on the deck that day. I brought her inside and put her in her room. A few days after this particular ordeal, she was talking to me and said that I wanted to cut her into small pieces. I was horrified! I calmly asked her when I had said such an awful thing. She explained it was when I put her out on the deck and she was kicking the door. I then realized that she interpreted my explanation of her possibly getting cut by the glass if she kicked it to me cutting her with the glass!

This was a revelation for me. I began to recognize how Virginia, and people in general, sometimes interpret what we say differently than how we intended it to be received. Motherhood is such a challenging job, and I still needed more training.

A few years later, Virginia was outside playing by herself and singing, which she did often. I sat down on the front steps to watch and listen to her sing. Virginia did not notice me on the steps. She was standing about thirty or forty yards away from me.

She looked up into the sky and said, "Please take me home; I don't want to be here." I knew she was talking to God. It broke my heart to hear her say something so heart-wrenching as, "Take me home, God." I couldn't understand why she would feel that way at such a young age. I personally never heard her say it at any other time, but I imagined that she might have felt that way often. I believe she may have felt this way because of the constant battles we had day after day. If something didn't go her way, or if I didn't give her a five-minute warning that we needed to leave for somewhere, a tantrum ensued. I believe she felt less loved because of this constant battle of the human will.

I kept a weekly and sometimes daily journal of how I was feeling about my life and the whole child-rearing experience. I often blamed myself for Virginia's outbursts and turned to God for help, promising myself I would not write about all the particulars of her behavior. Instead, I wrote about how I responded to the ordeals I went through each day. It was important to me that she wouldn't someday read all about the frustration I felt. I didn't ever want her to feel that she was to blame for it.

Some days, when the tantrums were taking a toll on me, I felt like I couldn't stand her. I know those feelings only came because I wasn't taking time out for myself to rest and regroup. I was also ignorant of how I should teach her to handle her emotions. I learned, over time, that many other mothers had similar feelings for their intense children. Over the years, speaking with other mothers who had spirited children, many of them confided in me their thoughts of not liking, or hating, their child. They had never told anyone before because they felt as guilty as I did.

It was not hatred of the child, but hatred of all the emotional strain and not knowing how to manage it. This realization that I was not the only mother who had feelings of dislike for my child began an eventual journey for me to forgive her and myself. I wrote down the positive things I felt when I looked at her while she was sleeping or when she was laughing and playing. I wrote about how badly I felt if I yelled at her or any of our children that day because I had allowed her to push me too far once again. Fifteen years later, I look back at those entries and recognize the growth that our whole family experienced in spite of the adversity.

Chapter Two
Six to Twelve Years Old

Realizing I Needed Help

There were a few other experiences similar to the one in the stroller when I snapped, lost my temper, and didn't handle the situation appropriately. One winter night, our four children and I built an igloo in our front yard. It was an amazing feat. The children were having a great time playing in the snow. Toward evening, as we were finishing up the inside of the igloo, I asked Virginia to do something and she refused. Wesley was fussing a little as well, but I was impatient and pulled him out of the igloo by his coat collar. Janessa recalled this incident and remembered thinking I was going to hurt Wesley. Janessa obviously could tell I was at my breaking point.

I didn't reason with Virginia either. I immediately lost my temper and grabbed her by the hair as she came out of the igloo. It left a bump on her head! I was horrified as soon as I realized what I had done. I ran to my bedroom and locked myself in. I sat on the floor wishing I could reverse time. I cried and sobbed uncontrollably. What was wrong with me?

As I wrote about this particular incident fifteen years after the fact, I began crying again as the dreadful memory came flooding back. I know we all make mistakes throughout our lives. Some of our choices or mistakes can harm others and may have long-lasting effects. This was one of those times when I made a choice that caused emotional pain to my older children who observed the ordeal and physical pain to Virginia. Even though Virginia forgave me and I eventually forgave myself, this was one of those stories that tore away at my heart for many years and still does.

I cannot even imagine what trauma I must have put Virginia and the rest of my poor little crew through. They all stood outside my bedroom door as I sat sobbing on my bedroom floor. They begged me to let them in. I refused at first. Janessa was intuitive and called my husband. Mark was away on military assignment in South Carolina and had been there for several months. He was activated by the Air Force and sent to Sumter, South Carolina after the 9/11 bombings. I heard Janessa talking to him and told myself that I would not talk to him no matter what. Dozens of thoughts rushed through my mind. What would he think of me? Janessa and John -Michael stood outside my door pleading with me to open the door, take the phone and talk with Daddy. I finally agreed to talk to him and started sobbing all over again as I told him what I had done.

He asked me if it would be okay if he called a friend of ours from our church. This friend was the women's pastor for our congregation. She also worked as a psychiatric nurse. I relented because I realized I needed help. After Mark called Tonya (name has been changed), she called and set up a time to meet with me. Tonya also talked me into finding a counselor who could talk with Virginia and me. When Tonya visited with me, she discovered the stress I was under, not only because Mark was away, but because of Virginia's behavior and what I was dealing with on a daily basis. She gave me some information to read about Oppositional Defiance Disorder (ODD). Tonya agreed that Virginia could have ODD because she had seven out of the ten symptoms mentioned in the document. I read this information over fourteen years ago. Researching ODD in 2016, I found that an updated list of symptoms of ODD is more severe now than it was when I read about them the first time. I found it interesting that the severity of the symptoms had worsened.

When Tonya, encouraged me to get some help with Virginia, it opened my eyes and I realized how important it was for me to find a counselor. Mark and I both needed to learn how to parent Virginia better. I felt I needed the counseling much more than Mark did because I lost my temper with Virginia more often than he did. I eventually found a wonderful counselor that some of my homeschool friends recommended. This counselor, Janet (name changed) lived several miles west of West Plains. Because she came so highly recommended, I was willing to try her out, in spite of the fact that we would have to drive over half an hour on windy country roads to see her.

Before I went to meet Janet, Mark and I videotaped a few of Virginia's tantrums. I thought I might need to show the video clips to Janet in case we needed some evidence of the severity of her tantrums.

The trip to Janet's home always made Virginia nauseous. By the time we arrived at Janet's home, Virginia was miserable and cranky because she felt sick. Once she got out of the car and walked around in the fresh air, she felt better and was willing to go inside.

During our first session, Janet met with Virginia for an hour and then met with me separately for an hour. She counseled us both an hour each week. She never asked to see the videos.

Virginia liked this counselor and opened right up to her. Virginia would go down into the basement where Janet had a little schoolroom set up with toys and learning activities. She played games with Virginia as they talked. At the end of the first visit, Janet handed me a cassette tape to listen to called *The Spirited Child* by Mary Sheedy Kurcinka, http:// www.parentchildhelp.com/

The next day I listened to the tape. I went and sat in

our bathroom and began crying uncontrollably. I suddenly realized that Virginia was not a rebellious child so much as she was spirited and intense. Later, I discovered other attributes/issues. I also realized Mark and I were not the only parents with a child as spirited as Virginia. This new knowledge gave me hope that she and I could both change. I researched this book more than fourteen years later and found amazing helps that I wish I had had when Virginia was tiny. I want to share what I found as you may find it helpful.

8 Signs You Have A Spirited Child

Does your child have convictions stronger than most star Olympians? Have they ever been voted "Most Likely to Star in a Broadway Production" by their preschool peers? Do your neighbors often wonder whether your kid has amputated a finger because their tantrums can be heard clearly from the next street over? If you answered "yes" to any of the above, you may be blessed with a spirited child. Here are eight signs that your kid is a kid with spirit.

1. Their perseverance perseveres, and keeps right on persevering. The spirited child wants what they want, and they will stop at nothing to get it.

Wow, this description fit Virginia to a T. The rest of these signs I will add here, but not all of them applied to Virginia.

2. They don't sleep like normal kids.

3. Their emotions are large and in charge.

Virginia's emotions were always large and in charge. I mention a few times in my story how I could find her in a crowd by just listening for her voice. She is still loud, but she has learned how to tone down the volume.

4. You've worried the neighbors are going to call the police. If you find yourself feeling concerned about what the neighbors think because your 4-year-old is screeching at ten thousand decibels after you politely requested that he put on pants, you may have a spirited child.

Thank goodness we lived out in the country when her tantrums were the worst. For five years, our closest neighbor was almost a half-mile away.

5. People have multiple theories about your child's behavior.

6. People have multiple theories about your parenting. You need to just ignore the tantrums and they will stop happening. You need to be more flexible. You need to practice relaxation exercises with them. You need to punish them.

7. They want to do it all.

8. They have a difficult time with transition. Do you dread leaving the house in sub-zero weather because you know your kid will actually need to wear shoes? Is getting them dressed each day like trying to wrangle and clothe a rabid wolverine? Have strangers at the grocery store questioned if you're kidnapping your own child because they are screaming in the parking lot? If you answered "yes" to any of the above, you may be the proud parent of a kid with spirit.

While life with a spirited child can be exhausting and frustrating at times, take solace in the fact that you could be raising a future leader of the free world. Perseverance, passion, and strong convictions are all positive qualities. The boundless cuddles and intense joy are also good perks. https://www.scarymommy. com/8-signs-spirited-child/ www.webmd

Indeed, raising a spirited child is exhausting. As the excerpt from the article states, spirited children have a hard time with transitions. Virginia had a tough time with transitions. I had to give her a five-minute warning when we needed to leave home, or just any transition at home. If I did not give her a five-minute warning, she had a break-down, kicking and screaming. I didn't always remember to give her the five-minute warning, though. When I forgot, I had to deal with a tantrum that would last at least fifteen to twenty minutes. She had learned how to manipulate as well. The manipulation I didn't recognize until our counselor in Jefferson City, Mrs. Jones, pointed it out several years later.

Janet, our counselor in West Plains, used play therapy with Virginia and, after only a month or two, I noticed some definite improvements in Virginia's behavior. She seemed more willing to do what she was asked without as many battles. Sadly, as we were just beginning to make progress, our family moved from West Plains to Jefferson City, Missouri. I did not find another counselor similar to Janet. I didn't have the internet resources available during that time that we do now to help me find a new counselor. I also was too embarrassed to ask for help from people at church. I felt like a failure as a mother if I couldn't resolve these issues on my own. Not only did I feel like a failure because of Virginia's behavior, but for my own lack of self-control. I periodically lost my temper when she pushed me too far. I also lost it because I was just worn out.

After we moved to Jefferson City, we went eight or nine months without a counselor. I finally decided to just find a counselor our insurance would pay for. The second counselor was a gentleman who worked for a local hospital. He diagnosed Virginia with a behavior disorder but didn't pin it down to any particular disorder. He never counseled with me or even asked to meet my husband. He only counseled with Virginia, which I realize now was why we didn't make any progress. Virginia met with him for three or four months with no improvement, so I stopped taking her to him.

At this point, she was nearly eight years old, and one particular evening she started yelling and screaming about something she wanted. Mark was home from work and stayed with our other children in the family room. I kept her in my room and sat against the door so she could not escape. I told her we wouldn't leave the room until she calmed down. She began yanking the covers off my bed and screaming at me. This went on for thirty or forty minutes. This was not unusual behavior for her.

In our congregation, I met a mother who had a daughter very much like Virginia who was an intense young lady. This mother was a nurse and explained to me how she started taking her daughter to a pediatrician when she was a toddler because she had horrible tantrums. My friend had been instructed to restrain her daughter so she would not hurt herself or others.

I was amazed how the Lord led me to this woman and learn about the need for restraining a child when her tantrums became too severe. I had already started restraining Virginia when she got out of control when I met this mother. Her stories of having to restrain her own daughter helped validate what I was doing with Virginia. I restrained her to keep her from destroying things or hurting others or herself. During the tantrum when she was pulling all the blankets off my bed, I chose not to restrain her. I sat against my door so she wouldn't run off and I began singing a children's hymn she knew. As I sang, she asked me "Why aren't you getting mad at me?" I responded that I didn't need to get mad. She yelled at me to stop singing. I asked why. She screamed, "If you don't get mad, you will not feel sorry for me!"

What? I thought to myself, she is doing this on purpose?

This was the beginning of a new road, a tough one but a new one. I finally came to the realization that she knew, if she pushed me hard and long enough, I would snap and yell or even spank her. Then I would feel so guilty and horrible that I didn't hold her responsible for her behavior because I was the adult and should not have lost my cool. This was a major breakthrough. Even though I finally realized that she knew what she was doing, it still took a few more years to understand how to parent her with this new understanding. I eventually received counseling to teach me how to parent Virginia, to learn to withstand the manipulation. And I realized it was just me. Mark only lost his temper with her two or three times. He was not as easily manipulated and she usually didn't fuss as often when he was around.

In 2017, I observed how even some autistic children use manipulation to their advantage to get what they want. A friend sent me a picture of her arm covered in bloody teeth marks from her seventeen-year-old child who screamed all kinds of obscenities at her and then hit and bit her because my friend told her "No." My friend wouldn't let her daughter run out of the house because this child would try to run off all the time. She told me her daughter didn't understand the dangers of cars on a busy highway. I can't imagine having to deal with a child that size. I know that even autistic children need to have boundaries set for them early in life. Both parents need to agree on how to handle volatile situations.

I kept journals about my life and wrote in them faithfully. Here is an excerpt from one of my journals when Virginia was eight.

Wednesday August 24th, 2005

"Virginia has really taken so much energy , but at least she is in school all day, and I get a break. Mark and I sat her down last week and set down some new rules. She doesn't get second chances until her behavior changes. We are basically starting at the beginning with her so that she learns not to manipulate anyone who has authority over her. This has become a challenge, but I have faith that it will work. And she will become even more precious than she is already."

As I read through these excerpts, I noticed how I didn't write the specifics of Virginia's behavior problems or issues. I only wrote a generic statement of what we were experiencing. I obviously had given in too much to the constant badgering and let her have too much leeway.

Virginia's first psychologist/counselor in Jefferson City referred us to a psychiatrist when I told him we wouldn't be coming back to visit him because I felt she wasn't making any progress. Our first meeting with the psychiatrist was in September of 2005. I found another journal entry that helped me pin down the date when we started seeing the psychiatrist.

September 22, 2005

"I took Virginia to a psychiatrist last week and I feel that we were able to pinpoint her problem. I hope and pray that now we can help her change and I must change, too, to make her change successful."

Interesting thing here from this journal entry. I didn't mention what Virginia's problem was that the psychiatrist pointed out. I also make the point that I too needed to change how I dealt with her and not just expect that if she changed it would solve the problem. I realized that I needed to change what I was doing as well.

After the first visit to the psychiatrist, Dr. Mick (name has been changed) diagnosed her with some kind of behavior disorder. I did not remember the psychiatrist pinning it down to a particular behavior disorder. I didn't write in my journal what that diagnosis was. That very first meeting he recommended she take an anti-anxiety medication. Sadly, I didn't even question why he would prescribe a medication as much as I should have. The anti-anxiety medication he prescribed was called BuSpar. He prescribed the five milligrams per day of BuSpar (buspirone hydrochloride). This is a phenomenally small dose compared to what is prescribed for children now. He also diagnosed Virginia with low-grade depression that he said she probably always had. Now this particular diagnosis might seem to make sense because of her expression a few years before that she wanted to go back to heaven and the information I mentioned about my depression and high emotions when I was pregnant with her. My depressed moods were not long-term nor did they last throughout my whole pregnancy. According to the data I shared earlier, she probably did not develop depression from me, but I am not certain.

I went home from the psychiatrist that day and read up on this particular anti-anxiety medication and its side effects, which included nausea, blurry vision, and many others. At the end of the list was suicidal thoughts. I looked up this medication fifteen years later and there is nothing about suicidal thoughts on the list. I found this fact interesting.

Virginia gained a considerable amount of weight while on the anti-anxiety/anti-depressant medications, which I later learned is a normal side effect for almost all people on these medications. I had a friend who worked as a nurse in Columbia, Missouri. She was taking antidepressants and she shared with me that these medications (SSRIs) caused her to gain ten to fifteen pounds of belly fat.

I was not concerned about Virginia's weight gain, although she gained weight around her middle, which I didn't notice until after we took her off the medication several months later. My concern was that it made her feel nauseous all the time. I discussed my concerns about the side effects, particularly the nausea and possible suicidal thoughts, with the psychiatrist. He said the dosage he put her on should not cause any problems.

I dutifully gave her the five milligrams of BuSpar per day. Nonetheless, she had nausea from the medication. I asked Dr. Mick about it at our next visit, and he said she would get used to the medication and the nausea would go away. After nearly five months on the medication, she still was nauseous! I told our psychiatrist that Virginia was still experiencing nausea. He didn't realize it had gone on for so long.

Because BuSpar made her nauseous, Dr. Mick changed her medication to ten milligrams of Paxil per day. She no longer had nausea while taking Paxil, which was a relief, so I didn't do any research about Paxil at the time. I naively trusted the psychiatrist and gave Virginia the medication according to his prescription.

Years later, as I began writing this story, I did some research on Paxil.

Here is a recent but not complete list of the different

side effects of Paxil, taken from Web MD. https://www.webmd.com/drugs/2/drug-32900/paxil-cr-oral/details/list-sideeffects

The following side effects are associated with Paxil CR:

- Cannot Empty Bladder

- Chronic Trouble Sleeping

- Diarrhea

- Difficult or Painful Urination

- Dizzy

- Drowsiness

- Excessive Sweating

- Feel Like Throwing Up

- Feeling Weak

- Head Pain

- Incomplete or Infrequent Bowel Movements

- Involuntary Quivering

- Loss of Appetite

- Nervous

Infrequent side effects of Paxil CR:

- Chest Pain

- Confused

- Feeling Restless

- Heart Throbbing or Pounding

- High Blood Pressure

- Muscle Pain

- Muscle Problems

In the following paragraph, I found more disturbing information about Paxil while researching, from the following website: http://www.antidepressantadversereactions. com/side_effects/hostility.php

"In June 2001, a Wyoming jury awarded 6 million dollars to the plaintiff in a case where a man killed his wife, daughter, baby granddaughter and then himself while under the influence of Paxil. The jury instructions and jury findings (in italics) were:

1) Can Paxil cause some individuals to commit suicide and/or homicide? (general causation): YES.

2) Was Paxil a proximate cause of these deaths? (specific causation): YES.

3) What amount of fault do you attribute to each of the following: SKB - 80%, Don Schell - 20%.

4) Damages - $8,000,000 [$6,000,000 to plaintiff].

These damages were assessed to SmithKline Beecham (now GlaxoSmithKline): Tobin v. SmithKline Beecham

Thousands of Americans are in prisons throughout the United States today because SSRI manufacturers have not only failed to tell the public that antidepressants can cause hostility and aggression, but have, behind their backs, participated in their prosecution.

If you, or someone you know, has become violent, aggressive or hostile while on an antidepressant, please report it immediately to the Federal Food and Drug Administration ("FDA"). This is very important because this is one way pressure can be put on drug companies to fully disclose the adverse side effects of their antidepressants. You can report your side effects at: https://www.fda.gov/Safety/MedWatch/default.htm by clicking on the Reporting Serious Problems to FDA box on the left side of the web page.

As I read the previous information during my research, I was shocked but not surprised. I chose this specific data because I knew from my own experience that Paxil can cause a person to act in ways that are unusual in comparison to their normal behavior, or sometimes more severe. Virginia experienced increased aggression and didn't complain about nausea while she was on Paxil, but had experienced nausea and headaches on the previous medication, BusPar.

As I researched this information, I realized I should have reported the aggression Virginia exhibited while taking Paxil.

Fifteen years later, I have learned more about antidepressants and their dangers. I have talked with several mothers over the years whose children were on some sort of antidepressant or a type of anxiety medication. Some of those mothers have lost their children to these drugs because of suicide or prison. The statistics of these medications are astounding. I am saddened by how many children are quickly prescribed and administered antidepressants. At the beginning of my journey of writing this book, a child of one of my friends was prescribed eighty milligrams of Prozac. Fortunately for him, his parents tried holistic paths and prayed for guidance before they placed him on SSRI's.

I feel that our lives are too busy and stressed that we cannot see what these drugs are doing to these young people, especially those who are in their pre-pubescent or puberty years. Not only do these drugs create havoc with their emotional system, but the liver has to work extra hard to deal with these toxins as they enter the body. Yet I do not discount the fact that many people can take these SSRIs without any of the terrible negative effects like I have experienced firsthand and learned about from other parents.

Years later, after Mark and I had already weaned Virginia off her medications and she had moved away from home to attend college, we counseled with a set of parents whose teenager had anxiety issues and had been prescribed

Chapter Two: Six to Twelve Years Old

antidepressants. As we observed this young teenager, I saw behavior patterns similar to those that Virginia exhibited. Those similarities were intense emotions, manipulation, hair twisting or fiddling with the hands (sensory issues), and a diet of too much sugar, bad carbs, and large amounts of processed foods. The young person's parents had taken their teenager off the antidepressants before I met them because of their concerns about the drug's side effects. When I met this teenager, he still struggled with intense emotions. I believe that if this teen could've been put on a strict diet of organic foods and no sugar the parents may have seen a dramatic change in his emotions.

I know that a clean diet doesn't solve every ailment, and some children do have chemical imbalances in their brains that can only be rebalanced through medication. I have met mothers who tried everything for their children before placing them on anxiety meds or antidepressants. One particular child inherited a behavior disorder from family members who had similar problems. When her mother started her daughter on the SSRIs, her behavior was as different as night and day, and the family was so relieved. I am not against SSRI medications completely. I also have a wonderful friend who takes SSRIs and has done so for more than ten years. This particular friend changed her diet over a year ago to a basic immune disorder diet and, since then, was able to cut her medication by two-thirds! I just want parents to research and try other options, particularly a clean diet, for a minimum of six months before turning to SSRIs.

The first medication, BuSpar, seemed to keep Virginia's emotions in check at first. Her tantrums were reduced from four or five tantrums per day to one or two per week. This reprieve lasted a few months and was a huge relief for all of us. Even after switching to Paxil, the tantrums were minimal for a short period. Up until this time, I had not realized how emotionally exhausted I was from the constant daily battles. The medications gave us rest we had not had for several years.

I had not learned how to always respond appropriately to Virginia's behavior up to this point. Doctor Mick recommended a counselor who was in the same medical facility he worked in. She worked across the hall from him. He recommended I seek her counsel to help me learn how to respond, rather than react, to Virginia. I agreed to meet with this counselor. She met with our whole family except Janessa, who was sick the day of our family meeting.

I found it interesting that Janessa later agreed to go to a counselor herself. I am sure that what Janessa experienced stemmed from the years of intense emotions in our home and our family dynamics. As Janessa's parents, we hadn't recognized the great amount of stress we had put upon her to watch after Virginia, let alone her other siblings. Janessa started babysitting when she was eleven or twelve years old. At this time during our child-rearing years, I had not learned how to handle Virginia's intense emotions. I realized later that it was unfair for me to put that responsibility upon Janessa all those years. Janessa has since graduated with her bachelor's in Psychology and may pursue a master's in social work. How ironic is that!

For the first few weeks, the new counselor met with Virginia. Then, after about a month of visits, she no longer met with Virginia. She began counseling with and training me how to parent Virginia. I needed to learn how to handle the emotions that bubbled up inside Virginia. Mrs. Jones (name has been changed) told me that Virginia would eventually grow to hate her. Mrs. Jones said, "Virginia will want you to stop receiving counseling from me." She explained that, if she was right about Virginia's behavior patterns, Virginia would eventually tell me how much she hated Mrs. Jones. This statement from Virginia indeed took place. One afternoon, I sent Virginia to a time-out and she yelled at me, "I hate Mrs. Jones. She has ruined our lives. Everything was fine until you started listening to her!" I was surprised that Virginia actually verbalized aloud her disdain for how I was trying to change my parenting with the counselor's help.

I was proud of myself at this time because Virginia's anger toward our counselor proved to me that Mrs. Jones was right and that I was headed down the right track. One of the key points Mrs. Jones taught me was to never let Virginia's emotions escalate. I was supposed to nip it in the bud as soon as I recognized that her emotions were about to rise. I didn't know how to do this at all at first. Even when I learned how to respond to Virginia, I didn't do it perfectly. Another key was that I needed to validate how Virginia was feeling and let her talk about it. All of us want to be validated and understood. As human beings, we do not want to be ridiculed for how we are feeling. We all have feelings whether they are right or wrong. I believe that, as human beings, we also want to be loved.

The knowledge our counselor gave me was empowering. Slowly I began to learn how to respond to Virginia's behavior. She was still taking Paxil when we began our counseling sessions with Mrs. Jones. Approximately three months into our counseling, Virginia's tantrums began to increase in frequency, intensity and severity. She was still on ten milligrams of Paxil per day. This would be the time when most psychiatrists would increase the dosage or switch to a different SSRI. Many individuals who take SSRIs become adjusted to the dosage of the SSRI and it is no longer helpful.

While Virginia's behaviors were escalating in frequency and intensity, our counselor taught me some other safe ways to restrain Virginia if she tried to hurt others or herself. Virginia had a few more tantrum episodes in which she tried to hurt herself and/or others. Usually the only people she tried to hurt were her siblings, and it was never severe, which is normal for most children.

At the end of each episode of restraining Virginia, she

and I were usually physically and emotionally exhausted. I asked the counselor what I should do when Virginia screamed that I was hurting her while I was restraining her. Mrs. Jones said that Virginia was trying to manipulate me and, if I didn't see blood, Virginia was fine. She instructed me to continue with the restraining until Virginia calmed down and agreed to listen. I should talk to her calmly and repeatedly tell her that I would let her go as soon as she stopped screaming and kicking, and calmed down. I remember wiping the sweat off Virginia's beet red face after each restraining ordeal.

Virginia screamed at me to let her go and that I was hurting her. Her hair was usually soaked by the time the episode ended. I often felt emotions of sadness well up inside of me. I had not yet learned how to master these ups and downs of her emotions. After one of Virginia's episodes, Wesley told me he was afraid of her. He also said he was afraid Virginia was going to hurt me really bad. Wesley was about five or six at the time. Up to this point, I was completely ignorant of the residual effects of Virginia's behavior. I hadn't realized how much this turmoil was affecting our other children. I take full responsibility for this and would love to go back and change things, something we all wish for at one time or another.

Before Virginia's worst episode occurred, we met with Dr. Mick. He said something during our session with him that day that seemed to influence Virginia into thinking her parents were wrong and he was on her side. I do not recall his exact words. He told Virginia something to the effect that he would be the referee if her parents were not handling her appropriately or doing the right things. He went on to say that parents sometimes make mistakes, and I agreed with that.

It was during this last session with him that something unusual happened. Virginia turned to look at me while he spoke with her. The look she gave me seemed full of hate, as if she utterly despised me. Right at that moment, I decided we should stop seeing Dr. Mick. The behavior she exhibited while we met with the psychiatrist that day was completely out of the ordinary. I can definitely say it wasn't her normal behavior while meeting with him. At home, she often got upset or mad about something and threw a tantrum, but she never before had shown this apparent disdain for me. With her usual tantrums, she would just cry and scream because she wanted something and I had said no to her demand.

A few days after this appointment with the psychiatrist, she had a very intense, violent tantrum that lasted approximately forty-five minutes. Unfortunately, I didn't remember to follow the exact sequence of steps Mrs. Jones taught me to use when Virginia started into this particular tantrum. There was something that day that Virginia wanted me to do and I refused. She screamed at me and it developed into a full-blown kicking, screaming ordeal. I asked Janessa to keep our youngest son upstairs until Virginia's tantrum was over. At one point while I was restraining Virginia, which involved holding her hands down to the ground and keeping her legs pinned so she couldn't kick me, Virginia looked me in the eye and, with a voice that didn't sound like her own voice at all, she said, "You will never win." I calmly replied that I had already won because I had not allowed myself to become angry. I remember those exact words between us as if it happened yesterday. It was an experience I will never forget. When I made that statement about not getting angry, she seemed to relax a little.

I had to continue the restraining, though, because she still tried to hit me if I started to loosen my grip. She actually broke away from me and ran toward the sliding glass door. Then she turned around and faced me, and I will never forget the look on her face. I saw in her eyes someone other than herself. She looked wild and crazed.

She lunged toward me, screaming like a wild person. She clawed at my face and ripped my shirt in the process. I was finally able to get control of her hands and legs again. I remained calm but came away bruised and scratched. This was the worst tantrum I had ever experienced with her. I have no doubt that some children who are on these medications are more susceptible to spiritual influences that are evil. I believe this because I saw it firsthand. I know what I saw. These medications take away a person's natural abilities to deal with and feel their own emotions. I can say this without any equivocation. The reason I can testify to this fact is I have a good friend who experienced a very similar situation with her own child who was on SSRIs.

I too have firsthand experience with this loss of feeling one's own emotions. I was prescribed an antidepressant many years before Virginia's huge tantrum. Mark and I had just moved our little family to Missouri. I became a little depressed after moving away from my family. My depression lasted for a few weeks. I learned that several women in my congregation at that time were also on SSRIs. I didn't see the harm in trying them.

I met with a psychologist and she was able to prescribe some antidepressants for me. I took the medication for three or four days. I could tell that I was losing the ability to feel my own emotions. I didn't like not feeling my emotions, so I quit taking the medication. I started taking an herb called Lady's Mantle instead. I do not deny the fact that many people that are prescribed antidepressants need them. Most of these individuals have clinical depression, are experiencing drastic life challenges, or have chemical imbalances outside of their control. I know the SSRIs these people are prescribed are necessary and very helpful for them. I have family members and friends that have taken antidepressants since childhood. Other family members have only taken SSRIs since they have become adults and usually after a very traumatic experience. I know for them these drugs have been and are a wonderful blessing. For others such as my daughter and the other youth you will read about in this book, SSRIs can cause worse and even deadly results after the initial calming effect takes place.

During this particular tantrum, when Virginia left me scratched and bruised, I believe it was one of the few times I didn't feel any sadness, anger or frustration toward her. I felt only compassion. Forty-five minutes after her tantrum began, we were sitting together on the floor of our family room. We were both tired, sweaty and emotionally drained. I held Virginia, rocked her in my arms, and kissed her forehead as she cried softly. A few minutes later, Virginia gazed on my bruised face and torn shirt. She asked me how I could still love her after what she had just done to me. The first thing I told her was that I loved her. I also explained that I forgave her because of what I knew and had learned about The Atonement of Jesus Christ, the Savior of this earth. I wanted her to know that I loved her and didn't ever want to give up on our quest to get her and our family through her developing years.

After this horrible ordeal, I made the decision to take her off the antidepressants and decided that we would do whatever it took to get through it. I didn't know when I made the decision how hard it would be. Here is another excerpt from one of my journals after we took Virginia off the medication. To this date (February 1, 2017), I have over twelve personal journals.

Wednesday October 17, 2007

"I didn't react this evening to Virginia; I responded. She may need to go back on medication though if she isn't able to deal with her emotions positively because it causes pain for the whole family. I pray that she will find some positive emotions within her and that they will dominate her negative emotions. I have faith she can do it if she will just try."

I see that I had such a hard time learning how to remain calm when she had a blow-up or tantrum but we kept at it. As Virginia grew older, she became more combative verbally. One of her common statements was, "You just want to control my life and you will not let me do what I want!" I believe this is a common statement from strong-willed and mild-mannered youth alike who want to do things their way. A young man I once counseled said the same thing to his parents. He had very similar behavior patterns to Virginia's when he was a young child.

A few days after the October 17, 2007, excerpt I wrote this in my journal.

Sunday October 21, 2007

"Today Virginia controlled herself amazingly well. I felt like our Heavenly Father had performed a miracle. Mark and I talked to her and she said she tried hard

because she wanted to play with Shelby again for longer periods, like last night. It was a blessing! Thank you, Heavenly Father, for this joy today!"

I noticed from this entry that I had written how Virginia was able to control herself if she wanted something bad enough and knew she had to earn it. Shelby was her best friend from third grade at Blair Oaks Elementary. They remained friends through high school and beyond. Every day after school during Virginia's fourth grade year, she wanted to spend all of her waking hours with Shelby. If I said she couldn't play with Shelby, she would argue incessantly with me. The problem with her spending long periods of time with her friend was that when she came home she would become more belligerent and less willing to do what she was asked.

January 28, 2008

"I just had to write that Virginia is doing much better, and she is controlling her emotions. She still has her outbursts, but they are much more mellow."

February 3, 2008

"Virginia turned eleven yesterday, she is doing better handling her frustration and I feel that I am doing much better too."

August 31, 2008

"Virginia is playing the piano well and is now in the sixth grade. Her behavior has improved amazingly well. Of course I have improved the way I respond, which is part of the problem."

Friday, December 19, 2008

"I am so thankful for the gospel and that our children have strong testimonies. Virginia's testimony is growing and she is doing amazingly well now. She has been off the medication for over a year now and she tries hard to control herself. We are truly blessed."

It was amazing to read through these entries and realize that with time she was learning how to control her emotions, and I was also improving my abilities in responding to her. She still manipulated me a lot and it took me many years to overcome that.

Tuesday, May 18, 2010, 5:45 A.M.

"Virginia's tantrums are so seldom now that it is a wonderful blessing. I think that she may have been hypoglycemic as a small child, but she hasn't been tested. Doctors may not be able to tell whether she was. She only whines during math and that is a blessing."

This last entry is interesting because I started to think about the possibilities of eating and food reactions as one of the possibilities for her behavior.

On February 14, 2011, at age thirteen, Virginia made a Valentine card for me and this is what she wrote.

"Dear Mom, I first would like to apologize for being so disrespectful to you in the past. I must admit that your core dedication has annoyed me in the past, but it has also taught me a great deal. I can't believe I have been so blessed as to have you for a mother. You are an amazing role model. No one could have a better one. I love you a lot. Happy Valentine's day. P.S. God loves you no matter what and so do I."

I was filled with so much joy as I read those old cards and journal entries and saw the growth that occurred in both Virginia and me. I am so thankful for the growth she experienced. We still had many ups and downs and arguments over the years.

At age thirteen, Virginia became a member of our Jefferson City Speech and Debate Club. This extracurricular activity was a great outlet for her intense emotions. With her speech and debate training, she began to debate with me about things she felt she had the right to do without my permission. I remember one of her comments, "Mom, that is just not logical thinking."

When I met with Mrs. Jones after Virginia's terrible tantrum, I told her I planned to take Virginia off Paxil and not return to Virginia's psychiatrist because of Virginia's increasing aggression. I explained Virginia's reaction to Dr. Mick during our last visit and stated I didn't feel she should continue seeing him. I believe Mrs. Jones was concerned about my decision but she did not discourage me from taking Virginia off the medication. She reminded me to wean Virginia off Paxil slowly and not to stop giving it to her cold turkey. She continued to guide me on how I should handle situations with Virginia. At some point during my counseling sessions, she told me that, in her twenty-five years of counseling, Virginia was the most manipulative person she had ever worked with. When she said this to me, I figuratively patted myself on the back as if to say good job, MaryAnn; you and Mark have hung in there through the tough times.

It is important for parents to remember that children become manipulative because their parents give in to their demands. If a child develops it at a very young age like Virginia did and the manipulation isn't squelched, it can lead to power struggles for years. Virginia developed this ability because I didn't get help from a pediatrician early on when she was sixteen months old. If I had realized this back then, I might have learned how to diffuse her tempers. I just thought she was stubborn. I refuse to beat myself up for not knowing what I should have or could have done then. I just want to help other parents get help and not feel embarrassed or afraid.

As time went on, I seldom handled Virginia's ongoing tantrums very well but I improved. Mark and I weaned Virginia off Paxil, but it was a horrendous ordeal. A month or two into the weaning process, Virginia had an intense tantrum. She did not react in the same way she had with the worst outburst while on Paxil, but it was an intense tantrum nonetheless.

I called Mark home from a pastoral visit he was making. This particular day he was out visiting some members of our congregation with our branch president/pastor. The two of them rushed home to help me. I was concerned that while I was restraining her that I had broken her leg. This, of course, was only a diversion to get me to let go of her. They returned and talked with her, but she was still combative and yelled at Mark in the process. It surprised me that she showed her intense emotions in front of our branch president. She eventually calmed down and Mark took our pastor home.

A short time later, maybe a week or so, I called Mark home from work, which I hadn't ever done before. Because Mark was in the United States Air Force when Virginia was in her early grade school years, he was away from home with his work for weeks and sometimes months. On this day, Virginia was having another terrible tantrum after we had taken her off Paxil. He returned home and had to restrain her. While he was restraining her, he told me to call the hospital, the psychiatric ward, because he was worried that we could not control her anymore. I picked up the phone, dialed the number but, as I waited for a human being to talk to me, I couldn't bring myself to complete the call. I hung up the phone and went back to Mark and told him I couldn't do it. I told him I wanted us to help her get through this ourselves. It took three or four months after taking her off the medication before her behavior leveled out to somewhat normal, which was one tantrum or two per day or every couple of days. It took a little over a year before the medication was out of her system.

Natural Foods

We continued to have rough days but nothing like it was before. As Virginia started to mature, she became a little more reasonable. At this time, I met an amazing mother of ten through our home school community. She was an herbalist and taught me a great deal about the effects of the food we eat on our emotions and physical development. This particular mother taught an herb class at our home school co-op that Virginia and I both attended. We both became very interested in learning more about herbs and natural foods. I started trying to keep the foods we ate a little more natural and use herbs rather than over-the-counter drugs for colds, etc.

We also stopped going to fast food places, which was usually less than once a week anyway. I didn't let our children drink soda except for special occasions, which were usually less than once a month. I still allowed them to eat white sugar in homemade cookies and cakes. We ate a good portion of processed foods like crackers and ice cream. Mark loves ice cream. I don't know if I could ever break him of that.

While our children were all still living at home, I hadn't developed enough of a conviction to take our family completely away from processed foods. I was barely beginning my education about the SAD (Standard American Diet) and how we needed to change our eating. I stopped eating processed sugars for two years from 2012-2014 and stopped drinking milk. That was during the time that my son John-Michael was serving his two-year mission for our church. To this day, I rarely eat processed sugar and, when I do, I feel tired and not as productive.

In the years that followed, weaning Virginia off Paxil, I often reached out to Pat, a friend of mine, about herbs. That friend has now passed on. During one of our lengthy conversations, she asked me if there were any foods I thought Virginia might be allergic to. I told her I didn't think there was anything because Virginia didn't have any symptoms indicative of someone with allergies. Pat said it was possible that her body was reacting to some type or types of food and it was affecting her moods and behavior. At that point, I didn't know anything about how food affects our moods. Pat was a master herbalist. She asked me if Virginia ate something excessively or more than other foods. I thought about it and concluded milk was something Virginia couldn't get enough of.

I learned more about natural healing and herbs and subconsciously decided to take Virginia off milk as much as possible. At the time, I couldn't find a farmer to sell us organic milk so I started buying skim milk. Skim milk cost less money and Virginia didn't like the taste of it. Thus, she wouldn't drink as much. Her behavior seemed to level out to a small degree. I noticed that when I bought two percent milk, Virginia would guzzle it down within a short time—an hour or less—she would become belligerent or argumentative. I didn't think the milk was bad for her, but I began to recognize that her body and emotions reacted to it somehow.

I realized later on that the milk wasn't causing an allergic reaction; she was probably experiencing a carbohydrate high. Most people who overload on carbs get that sugar rush, then plunge back down into a depressive or ornery mood. I have spoken with several other mothers who have or had children with Virginia's same characteristics and behavior patterns. These mothers told me how their son or daughter would eat a whole bag of potato chips or a half a gallon of ice cream in one sitting, or just a variety of high carbs. Usually these food items were also high in trans fats and/or sodium content. These children and youth all seemed to have the same diet preferences and the same emotional intensities as Virginia experienced and displayed. I came to the conclusion that Virginia and other youth like her crave or become addicted to these carb highs. The lows after the carb high exacerbates their intense personalities and brings out the defiant, sexual (in some of them I met), argumentative, or depressed behavior.

These carb loads may not affect everyone this dramatically as these children with intense behaviors. From my observation of high sensory personalities/spirited children such as Virginia, they crave these high carb foods. I believe my mother-in-law had addictive or high sensory behaviors as a child and carried it through into her adult life. She started smoking at age eleven and drank excessively as she grew older. My husband said she was not an alcoholic; she drank alot. But he was only aware of her excessive drinking during his teen years. My mother-in-law's own mother, Sylvia, told me that her daughter was good until she was two. In other words, after age two, Virginia Lammi wasn't good anymore. I didn't understand what Sylvia meant when she shared this with me many years before I even had children.

Years later, as my children grew and developed, I remembered Grandma Sylvia's words. After my mother-in-law passed in 2000, I longed for her help with Virginia. I believed she might have understood our little girl and may have known how to help me. Sadly, my mother-in-law, whose name was Virginia, passed away when my daughter was only three and a half.

A year or two after we took Virginia off Paxil, I met an amazing woman I will call Lisa. She reminded me so much of my mother-in-law it was uncanny. Lisa was a fabulous cook and seamstress, as was my mother-in-law. She was a smoker, just like my mother in law, but she never smoked in front of our children. My mother-in-law never smoked in front of our children, either. In fact, there was only once that Janessa smelled smoke on her grandma's breath. Grandma Ginny told Janessa never to start smoking because it is a terrible habit.

My friend Lisa had a feisty personality just like Grandma Ginny and that is probably why she connected so well with Virginia. I asked Lisa if she would teach our children how to crochet. She agreed to teach Virginia and Wesley. She was very patient in the teaching process and never put up with any guff or smart mouth from our children, and I loved that about her. I met her in 2006; she passed away in 2016. We visited Lisa almost every Thursday for nearly six years. She loved Virginia and Virginia loved her. She not only taught our children how to crochet, she taught them to tie quilts, cook and respect her. She was an answer to unsaid prayers.

Lisa was a fantastic cook and my children loved her cooking. One of her specialty sandwiches was cream cheese and black olives on cinnamon raisin bread, which is very tasty. Lisa could get our children to try any food dish she made. I would call her for advice about parenting, not just Virginia, but all my children. I even asked her for marriage advice. She always gave me wonderful counsel. She taught Virginia how to get along with her little brother, even though Virginia didn't always follow that counsel.

I remember when Lisa sat down with Virginia and asked her how she was treating me or her little brother and talked to her about what it means to really apologize. Virginia was respectful to her and, if she wasn't respectful, Lisa called her on it and immediately Virginia apologized.

I believe it is vital to look outside our own families for help and support. It is important to find individuals, counselors or groups that have the same values and standards as our own so they can relate to us and our children.

Virginia was away on a church mission when Lisa passed away. When I sent Virginia the news of Lisa's passing, she told me she went to a quiet place and cried over the loss of this great friend and mentor in her life.

Music was an avenue of emotional release for Virginia. She started piano lessons at age six or seven and progressed quickly each year. During her second or third year of lessons, she argued with me about practicing. Some days she started screaming right there at the piano and screamed sometimes for half an hour while sitting at the piano. I was tired of the battles and let her quit lessons for several months. Eventually Virginia came to me and asked if she could restart her lessons. I asked her teacher Dr. G for some advice. She told me she would have Virginia sign a contract with a promise to practice and not give me any push back about practicing. I felt this would be the answer. Virginia signed the contract and she never complained much after that. It worked! Virginia continued piano lessons up through her sixteenth year, then quit. I didn't want her to quit her lessons, but I needed to allow her that choice. Her teacher assured me that Virginia had enough training to continue doing well with her piano so I let it go.

Before high school, I found another avenue for Virginia to focus her energies on—our local homeschool speech and debate club. She grew into a great speaker and debater. She could debate with me over any issue as her skills improved. She started with this club when she was only twelve years old. She excelled and improved with each successive year. As a sophomore, she progressed to compete in the National Speech and Debate competition in Arkansas. Virginia competed with a persuasive speech about parenting that she authored. With this speech she won 8th place overall. She was so excited and we were very proud of her. The following year she convinced Wesley to compete with her. She took the story "The Boy in the Striped Pajamas" and condensed it into a dramatic duo. They were fantastic. They took first place at almost every competition. Sadly, we didn't go to Nationals that year, even though they qualified, because of finances. They spent hours practicing and they often fought during the process because Virginia wanted to do it one way and Wesley didn't want to do it at all. But they were successful in their endeavors. Wesley usually relented to do it the way Virginia insisted it should be done.

I homeschooled each of our children up to high school, but I enrolled Virginia in public school in third grade because I really needed the mental break. When she was in her fourth grade year of public school, I realized that if she continued in the public system she might hurt someone or get kicked out. I came to this conclusion one day after she told me how she was going to tell her teacher how stupid she was because she let kids do things Virginia didn't agree with. She was nine years old at the time!

I believe it is essential for families that have children with these intense behaviors to have family counseling and therapy. The whole family is affected when you raise spirited children and professional counselors have taught me so much. It is not just the child that needs help or training. The parents and family need help counseling and training too.

Chapter Three

Thirteen to Twenty Years Old

Virginia Learns to deal with Her Intense Emotions

When Virginia was thirteen, I hired a voice teacher for her. She had always loved to sing. She must have developed amazing lungs from all those hours of screaming as a small child. When she was still under five years old, she would sit on her bed and line up her dolls and sing to or with them. In her pre-teens, her older brother used to discourage her from singing so loud in church. I am sure it must have been embarrassing to him that everyone looked at us when she sang. But, as her older brother matured, he was the first to champion her when she sang at an event. One particular performance, Virginia was the youngest on stage and when she finished her vocal piece, John- Michael stood up and yelled "That is my sister!"

On one of our trips to Utah, which we usually took every

year, one of my older brothers, Stephen, had the opportunity to hear her sing the national anthem. She was not quite eight years old at the time and my brother asked if she would sing in his congregation's Sunday meeting the next day. It was close to the Fourth of July and so she sang the Star Spangled Banner. She agreed to do it even though she was very nervous. She received a great deal of praise after the meeting. As she grew older, I began to realize that she had an amazing voice. She has a powerful voice and perfect pitch. I know that her singing was a great outlet for her intense emotions.

She took piano lessons for six years and guitar lessons for one year. After she started the voice lessons and guitar, she began writing music. She wrote over a dozen songs while she was just learning to play guitar. At this point, I believe she has written more than twenty-five songs. She sang up to four hours every day. Wesley was so tired of the singing that, when he traveled in the car alone with me, he didn't want to listen to the radio.

The songs Virginia wrote were usually about relationships with boys or family, specifically fathers. Some of her songs were very mournful but they always had a message of some sort. I know that this singing hour after hour was a daily outlet for her intense feelings and emotions. Someday I believe she will publish all the songs she has written. I look back now and realize that the music, singing lessons, and speech and debate team were great outlets for her energy and intensity.

Even though we still had some rough times in Virginia's teenage years, we never went back to the antidepressants. There were times in her teen years when she regressed back to her foot stomping, toe crunching, and screaming. She never became violent again as she had while she was on the antidepressants. One particular day, while we lived in the St Louis area, she wanted to go see a boyfriend of hers. She wanted to drive there by herself. She was sixteen at the time. I said no. She raised her voice and began to argue and reason with me. She debated with me why I should allow her to go. She even started crunching her toes on the floor like she used to as a small child. I couldn't believe this was happening and I felt a surge of dread come over me. I finally gave in. I was tired of the badgering, and told her she could go if she took her younger brother with her. She didn't like the idea, but she agreed. I know I shouldn't have given in but I was grateful that we were able to at least come to a compromise that I could feel a little better about. I believed her brother would let me know if she broke the rules.

As the years passed, I began to realize how fortunate we were as a family to have gone through those tough years of trial when she was young. I do not think I would have had the courage to take her off the medication if we had not been through the intense adversity during the earlier years of her life. I already knew what it was like not to have her on medication up to age eight, and we had lived through those eight years. This knowledge and my faith in God gave me the courage to forge ahead and begin the journey of the next eight years. I believed, after taking her off the medication, that we could get through whatever lie ahead, with God's help. It was never easy but it was worth it.

A friend asked me recently if I could change anything about how I raised Virginia with the knowledge I have now, what I would do. My first response was: I would have taken her to a pediatrician when she was sixteen months old to find out if her intense behaviors were normal and how I should deal with them, and I would have gone to a family counselor earlier to teach me how to stop the manipulation. Also, I would have started our family on a natural food diet to help change her body's responses to food. Our emotional health has so much to do with the food we eat. This next excerpt from an article about nutritional psychology, really highlights for me the correlation between our emotions and food, specifically unhealthy food.

Like an expensive car, your brain functions best when it gets only premium fuel. Eating high-quality foods that contain lots of vitamins, minerals, and antioxidants nourishes the brain and protects it from oxidative stress—the "waste" (free radicals) produced when the body uses oxygen, which can damage cells.

Unfortunately, just like an expensive car, your brain can be damaged if you ingest anything other than premium fuel. If substances from "low-premium" fuel (such as what you get from processed or refined foods) get to the brain, it has little ability to get rid of them. Diets high in refined sugars, for example, are harmful to the brain. In addition to worsening your body's regulation of insulin, they also promote inflammation and oxidative stress. Multiple studies have found a correlation between a diet high in refined sugars and impaired brain function — and even a worsening of symptoms of mood disorders, such as depression.

It makes sense. If your brain is deprived of good-quality nutrition, or if free radicals or damaging inflammatory cells are circulating within the brain's enclosed space, further contributing to brain tissue injury, consequences are to be expected. What's interesting is that for many years, the medical field did not fully acknowledge the connection between mood and food.

Today, fortunately, the burgeoning field of nutritional psychiatry is finding there are many consequences and correlations between not only what you eat, how you feel, and how you ultimately behave, but also the kinds of bacteria that live in your gut. https://www.health.harvard.edu/blog/nutritional-psychiatry-your-brain-on-food-201511168626

While our children were young, we ate the SAD "Standard American diet." We ate plenty of sugar and processed foods, including healthy homemade foods as well. I can see now how much our emotions are affected by what we eat on a daily basis.

The years of Virginia's tantrums were extremely trying for everyone in the entire family. One particular time, when Janessa was left in charge to babysit, Mark and I went out on a date. Virginia and Janessa fought so badly that Janessa refused to ever "babysit" again. But, over the years, they have all grown and matured. We now have a stronger bond between us. I do not have any doubt that, if we had continued with the anti-anxiety meds in her earlier years, she would have ended up hurting herself or someone else. I believe this to be true because of the experience I had with her during her last major tantrum while still on Paxil.

Virginia started college at age seventeen. I drove with her to Brigham Young University in Idaho, which is over fourteen hundred miles from our home in Missouri. We had an enjoyable trip. We traveled to Idaho with Janessa, who would be Virginia's roommate. A friend of Janessa's drove out with us as well. When we arrived in Rexburg, Idaho, we unloaded all Virginia's things into her dorm and met her roommates. I am sure she was nervous.

At the end of the orientation day, it came time for me to say goodbye. I choked up with tears and hugged her. I hadn't expected this reaction from myself. I was ready for her to be out on her own! I was ready to have the break. Most parents experience a bit of these same emotions when they send their children off to college for the first time. I thought I would be ecstatic that Virginia was out of the house. So these feelings of sadness as she walked away were confusing. Janessa, who was standing there with me at the time, said something to me that truly hit home. "The children who take the most emotion and work to raise are often the hardest ones to let go." She was absolutely right.

That first semester at college was an adventure for Virginia and I know she loved her newfound freedom. Janessa was a great exemplar and expected Virginia to obey the university's rules and regulations. It is a religious university and there are stricter rules there than on your average campus.

At age nineteen, Virginia began a year-and-a-half proselyting mission for our church. She had many ups and downs in the first five months. She learned so much about herself. I added some of her letters from that time as well as a few shorter excerpts to show how much she changed. She still struggled with depression at times during her service but she pushed through. There is hope for families everywhere who feel there is no alternative other than medications.

As a parent raising an intense, spirited child, it can be overwhelming or even seem impossible. I know that training these amazing children through those intense years can be done, and parents mustn't ever blame themselves for making mistakes. Our first counselor asked me straight out if I blamed myself for Virginia's behavior. I answered in the affirmative. It took several years before I learned how to stop blaming myself for her behavior patterns and for the myriad of mistakes I made when I lost my cool. Everyone can learn to stop blaming themselves with help and/or positive counseling. For me, it took not only counseling but a lot of prayer as well. For those who believe in God or a higher power, I strongly recommend implementing prayer into your daily routine.

It is an ongoing journey

I realized that it may help others to include some of Virginia's own words to my writing, especially those from her early adult years. Here are a few letters from Virginia's proselyting mission to show the journey she continues to travel. She served her mission in Las Vegas, from March 2, 2016- September 20, 2017. This was the first email we received from Virginia after she left for her eighteen-month mission. The names have been changed to protect identities.

March 4, 2016

Hello everyone!

Today we were so blessed to be able to email even though it is not our Preparation day. P-days will be on Thursdays while I am here at the MTC-Missionary Training Center.

Well...when a friend of mine told me that the MTC was like trying to drink water from a fire hydrant he was right! I feel like I have had so much information crammed into my head in just the last few days. At times I have even felt like the teachers have been beating me over the head with the same concept. But I know that it is so it will be ingrained upon our hearts and our minds.

I have two companions so I am in a trio! They are fabulous! One sister is short and perky. The best way I can describe her is like a Chihuahua. Always talking, always bouncing, always positive. Sister B is the complete opposite. She is quiet most of the time. I feel like I fit somewhere in the middle. My relationship with them has improved as I have looked for what I can learn from them instead of what I can teach them. It has opened my eyes to what wonderful and amazing sisters they are. And they are so sweet and complimentary of me.

Our district is great! We only have four elders and then us three sisters. Sister B and Elder Jones are going to the Nevada, Reno mission but everyone else is going to Las Vegas.

I have already been called as the Senior Companion and Sister Training Leader. Yay for new responsibili-

ties...haha. I know I will only grow and learn from the opportunity and experience.

Now I promised myself I would be very honest in my emails, staying positive, but also being honest when I'm struggling so others can know that it is completely normal to feel inadequate and behind. And, boy, do I feel inadequate! Every time I think I've got it or I know something or how we should plan a lesson, I am corrected. Which is good! But today I had to try really hard not to break down in tears in front of my teacher Brother Fish and my companions when I felt like I am never gonna get how to plan right and teach with the Spirit. I know that I will come to know how to as time goes on and as I practice more and humble myself. Besides, it's only been the third day!

Well, this is only supposed to be a short email (whoops, got carried away!) so I will talk to you all later next Thursday!

With loads of love,
Sister Virginia Bradley (women are called sisters)

P.S. I know this is the Lord's work and that He has (and will) qualify his servants for it.

Also, here is my address while I am here at the MTC

if any of you would like to write me letters or send packages! Those always brighten days (wink wink).

These emails home from Virginia made me laugh so hard and cry as I observed the growth and struggle she experienced. We become stronger through adversity. Weight lifting is a great analogy with adversity making us stronger. The muscles experience slight tears through weight training but, as the training continues over time, muscles rebuild themselves and become stronger and larger. As our family worked through challenges, including raising challenging children, we have become stronger and hopefully more humble and willing to listen to other's advice and ask for help.

Here are a few more letters from Virginia. Take notice of the growth over time, the positive nature of her letters, and how upbeat she was with what she wrote. I cried many times over her letters as I saw the hand of God at work in her life. She still had her rough days and related how she struggled with depression. This emotional struggle within her is like any weakness many of us struggle with. There is a scripture I would like to refer to concerning weaknesses. "And if men come unto me I will show unto them their weakness. I give unto men weakness that they may be humble; and my grace is sufficient for all men that humble themselves before me; for if they humble themselves before me, and have faith in me, then will I make weak things become strong unto them." Ether 12:27; The Book of Mormon, another Testament of Christ. The following email was sent after she left the missionary training center in Provo, Utah, and became involved in the work in Las Vegas, Nevada.

May 9, 2016

Helloooooo!!!!

Wow, this week has been amazing! Tuesday and Wednesday were crazy because my companion got transferred Tuesday morning but my new companion didn't come to Vegas until Wednesday night. So I was with so many different sisters and members to make sure I never was without a companion or left alone. (Missionaries always have to be with a companion.) Wednesday was a hard day. One of our investigators dropped us, another avoided us, and it was hot and I three-packed it with the new sister training leaders and felt like I was doing everything wrong. I almost decided to come home...again, haha!

But then I pulled myself together for my new companion. I thought to myself, "This is going to be her first night in the field. I can't mess it up." So I put a smile on! And it hasn't left my face since.

Sister Villalobos is heaven sent. She is the cutest little ray of sunshine I could've ever asked for! It has amazed me how easy it is to love being a missionary when you have a companion who encourages you, laughs with (and sometimes at) you, and is positive! It is like I am serving in a totally new area. I feel like a different person. I've realized that attitude really does make the difference. Instead of tearing each other down and constantly being critical, we build each other up! When we see someone we make a beeline for them! Both of us together. We whisper to each other and we walk like we fear no man! And let's baptize them! Future missionaries right there, let's go! Then after we talk to them we say something positive about the experience, regardless of whether or not they were receptive or flaming anti's who have nothing nice to say. I really cannot tell you how things have changed.

Our teaching pool is the biggest it's ever been! We had more people at church than ever before! Miracles are happening. Because we have the faith to make them happen and we smile and tell ourselves we love doing this until it is true. Attitude. Is. Everything.

Some cool experiences this week...

We were street contacting and knocking on potentials' doors and then it started down pouring! But we just laughed! We jumped over puddles and got soaking wet. But Sister Villalobos said "Yes! I love it! I always wanted to rough it in the rain!" Temple Square sisters look forward to their outbound missions forever. They don't get to meet their investigators or members face to face. So this experience for them is what they have yearned for and waited for their whole missions! That enthusiasm is electric. Because she is enthusiastic, I feel like it is okay to be enthusiastic, too! Thus we find so many more people and have such a good time together.

Sister Villalobos is afraid of dogs. So once we knocked on a door and when they opened it, their dog ran out. Sister Villalobos grabbed the male church member who had come out with us and shoved him in front of her and held onto his waist while hiding behind him. Haha! It was so funny! He thought so too! She is getting better though. I don't know how she survived in Guatemala! There are tons of dogs there.

We were going to visit a potential and as we were walking down the street, I felt like we needed to knock on this door. So we crossed the street and knocked on the door. As I peeked inside, it was obvious that no one was home. So I wondered to myself, "Why? Why did I feel impressed to knock on this door if no one was home?" Then I had the thought "Because you needed to stop and wait so you could be in the right place at the right time later." We continued walking. We came upon this beautiful view of the valley and stopped to take pictures. A man on a golf cart was driving up the hill. So we waved at him and so he stopped. Of course who wouldn't when two cute girls are waving at you? Just kidding ;) He was from Mexico so Sister Villalobos hit it off with him right away. He agreed for his ENTIRE FAMILY to meet with us!! The Lord truly has impeccable timing! Miracles can happen and we can find the people who are prepared for the gospel and who need US (not just as missionaries but as friends and neighbors) when we listen to the Spirit and we don't fear man!!

Sister Villalobos is helping me with my Spanish. It isn't very good. But I am getting better! I think she likes to help me because it is so funny when I mess up! Haha!

We are all supposed to be here on this earth at this time. WE HAVE PURPOSE. God made you and me wait until now. Why? Well, I guess it's up to each and every one of us to find out :) One thing I do know. This gospel is real. There is more than this life. There is more than just how much money you can make, how many people you can date, and how skinny you can become. Who. Flippin. Cares. When I stand before God, just like Sister Hinckley, I want to look rough. I want Him to know that I used myself up, wore myself out, and did all I could to help those around me. If you aren't tired by the end of the day, you didn't do enough! We can all do more! And, if you feel discouraged or depressed, remember that we usually only feel overwhelmed and like that when Satan is attacking us and when we are focusing on ourselves. When we focus on the joy of being able to help others, to love, and serve, and get to know, and become more like Christ, the world is brighter. Don't believe me? Maybe it only works for some people? Come on, seriously? You are fooling yourself. Put it to the test.

I love you guys so much!! But I am learning to love the Lord more.

When we give all that we have to the Lord, it is amazing how much more we have to give to others :)

Adios!
Sister Virginia Bradley

The positivity in this previous letter was so uplifting. She has learned how our attitude about life makes all the difference. She worked really hard to improve her attitude and it helped her so much to become paired with a companion who could help her feel positive about life and her mission.

When I saw the title to Virginia's next letter, I was concerned. I was worried that she was going to give up and come home. Read it and smile.

August 22, 2016

I can't do this!

So this week has been awesome!! Although I did have a slight mental/physical breakdown right after Sister Hope went to the doctor! How ironic! But some extra sleep took care of that. The next day I sat pondering on my little panic moment the day before. And I came to the conclusion that I most certainly without a doubt cannot do this! I'm too weak, too stubborn, too prideful, too imperfect! Inside I knew it was true. I would simply exhaust myself again if I kept doing this. I would hit rock bottom again. Because I simply am not strong enough. I accept it. I acknowledge it. But just as sure as I knew I could not do this, I knew someone else could. My Savior already suffered rejection, disappointment, self-doubt, weakness, sin, everything that brings me down! And He overcame it all.

So it's true I most definitely cannot do this. But my Savior can, He already did. So all I have to do is lean on Him. Not just lean but depend! Then and only then will I be able to do what I've been called to do. As I came to that realization, a peace came over me. With Jesus

Christ, I can do this. I can be the missionary He wants and needs me to be. On my own? Not a chance! But with Him? That's the only chance. I know it is the same for all of us. When we give it all to the Lord. When we humble ourselves enough and realize that no amount of money, education, brains, talent, ability, training, or will power will suffice. WE NEED THE SAVIOR. That's why He came! To save us! How unbelievably and incomprehensibly grateful I am for Him. I encourage you to make your relationship with Jesus Christ your priority. When we do that, we are enabled and empowered. Don't you want that in your life? So aside from my personal travails we had other miracles! Our investigator Jamie came to institute (which is like a Bible study). He loved it! We were so happy! Then we had four people come to church! It was certainly an exciting day. It was amazing to see them feel the spirit. Because this is Christ's church here on the earth again with His priesthood authority directing it, the feeling we get there is unparalleled. And our friends noticed that. Sorry this is short this week! But I gotta eat my potstickers. Hahaha! Some things never change.

I love you all! And want you to know that I love the Lord. I love this gospel and I love this work. There really is nothing better than building the kingdom of God among our friends and families. Keep the faith, brothers and sisters! One day we will stand on Mount Zion with the Lord and being faithful will have all been worth it. I know it will.

Love!
Sister Virginia Bradley

P.S. The title gotcha, didn't it? Hahahaha!

Notice that she said she was too stubborn. I can wholeheartedly agree about the stubborn part; she was indeed! The positive attitude continued but she still had times when she was down. The following letter was a personal letter to Mom (me) and how she struggled with depression/emotions again. I noticed more after she matured and moved away from home how her emotions were usually lowest when she was ill or wasn't exercising and/or eating unhealthy.

August 2016

Dear Mom,

I had some pretty low points again where I just wanted to put on my jeans, pack up my bags and run away somewhere where no one would ever find me or know me. I wanted to just disappear. But clearly I didn't do that. :)

I love you, Mom. As I told Dad, I'll be fine, don't

worry. I've been doing better on being more obedient, which I think was mostly why I was feeling so much self-loathing. But I still don't feel super in tune with the Spirit. I guess that's another challenge, still doing spiritual things even when you don't feel it. Just keep on, keepin on!

I love you so much! And thanks for the pictures and videos. I'm glad Wesley made JV.

Love,
Sister Virginia Bradley

I wanted to add another letter that Virginia sent in 2017. I noticed even more growth in her spiritually and emotionally as I compared this letter to the letter from August 2016. I loved reading about how she had had a rough day and she cried and ate chocolate. So read on and see for yourself the growth that continued to happen as she matured and received greater responsibilities.

January 23, 2017

Dear friends and family,

This past week went by very quickly! But was also full of long days. As leaders, we are expected to set the example. It is expected for us to have good numbers (remember, there are people behind the numbers).

*I once heard a statement that people are what you
expect of them or they become what you treat them as.
Something like that. I have been amazed to see that
come to fruition. As I have risen to the new standard
expected of me, I realize the power in empowerment.
We should always expect and encourage the best from
others. In treating them as if they are their best selves
they will become such.*

*We had a leadership meeting this week with all of the
zone leaders and Sister training leaders in the mission.
Man, oh, man, did I feel overwhelmed! But we must
remember that when we are called we are called by the
Lord. He knows us. He knows what we are capable of.
And he knows where we need to grow. So don't panic!
Embrace it and do your best while trusting in the Lord.*

*One evening, we were with a young woman on our
way to a return appointment with a guy we had met the
previous day. When we got there, he and his neighbor
were drinking and smoking to some chill music in his
driveway. We walked up and began to talk with them.
Very quickly, the neighbor began to tell us how we
were wrong doctrinally and how we were trespassing,
etc. We gave it our best shot to teach them something
and bring the spirit in. But, man! When people are
under the influence, there is just not much you or
anyone can do. (Thank you, Lord, for the word of*

wisdom that keeps us away from such nonsense!) I and Sister L. steadily became more and more fed up with their rudeness and their embarrassing foolishness. So I asked, "Is there a time we can come back when you're not drunk?" Both of the men gasped! One said to the other "Are you drunk?" "No!" replied his friend. "Didn't think so," he concluded. Sister L. was trying so hard not to laugh out loud. As we walked away, all three of us laughed away our frustration.

Despite lots of meetings, cold rain and wind, we have been able to have a very productive week! I know that, even when we are incredibly busy, if we will work our hardest at the Lord's work, He will make the time that we do have effective. More effective than if we had shirked responsibilities and done whatever we wanted. Just like with tithing! If we will have faith and give the ten percent the Lord requests then He will bless us to do more with the nine tenths remaining than we could've done with the full ten.

Lately I have been studying the New Testament from beginning to end instead of just topics. It has been a beautiful experience that I have fallen in love with. Studying more about the Savior has given me comfort and strength and increased my faith! I encourage you to each day take some time to study about our beloved Savior.

Now, in case you are mistakenly thinking that life is just peachy for me, it's not. I did spend a whole lunch hour in my bathroom crying and eating chocolate as I sat on the floor the other day. But the important thing is what we focus on and how we react to the struggles we face. My study of the Savior has reinforced my habit to turn to Him when I'm struggling and to rely on Him through the trial. We must look at the positive and press forward. It's really that simple.

We went and visited a man this past week who our record of him wasn't very hopeful. But we tried anyway. Come to find out he was not of the attitude he had been previously and readily accepted our invitation to teach him. I know that people change and life happens. So we never know when those around us may be ready for the gospel. What we must do is be there and never give up!

As we were walking around in one neighborhood, we stopped by this home looking for someone specific. As family members came home, we asked them if so and so was there. They were less than cordial and walked past us into their home. Later we walked down the same street and we met their neighbor, who was a very warm and friendly woman who welcomed us to return and share our message.

Now we could've allowed the previous experience to sour our mood and cause us to leave that street. But we continued to work and talk to people. In doing so, we found someone who was willing and ready to learn. Ether 12:6. Don't quit prematurely! Actually, don't quit at all! You never know what the Lord has in store for you.

Love ya all! And miss ya all, too! Keep smiling, praying, and seeking learning at the Savior's feet. This is a glorious time we live in and a marvelous journey we have embarked on.

Love,
Sister Bradley

It is so impressive to witness the growth that I have seen take place in Virginia in the nineteenth and twentieth years of her life. Parenting is an ongoing process of learning how to teach our children even as they become adults. We have to learn how to allow others to mentor and teach them. This can be hard sometimes; it has been for me. I know that I was a control freak as a parent when our children were younger. I also noticed this need for control in other families.

Several years ago, I had an experience with an adult who appeared to be upset by my involvement in their child's life. That particular child would come to me for advice and counsel instead of their parent. At first, this caused tension between the parent and me but, with time, the waters settled and our relationships improved. From that experience, I told myself that I would allow our own children to have adult mentors and be thankful for them. As a parent, I often wanted to just fix the child's problem. I often wanted to take Virginia in my arms and tell her it would be okay. I do know that stepping back after a child asks for advice to see how they will follow your advice or disregard it has always been and continues to be challenging for me. I am what my husband calls a helicopter parent.

Even though it was hard when I heard that Virginia had had a hard week—or several weeks—while on her mission, or felt depressed, I knew she could get through it. We made it through so much when she was young, and I believe her past gives her more incentive to push through. Virginia has survived my lack of parenting skills and I am sure will do better with her own children. Mark really knew what to say to her during some of the hardest months on her mission. He is blessed with a great gift to counsel her and others with love. He knew the right things to say that would comfort and encourage her. I do not know if she will always struggle with bouts of depression, but we all get depressed to some degree at different times in our lives. I have no doubt that Virginia can make it through anything now. The service she gave while on her mission has taught and will continue to teach her so much patience and perseverance.

I have loved reading Virginia's emails from her mission.

They always brought a smile to my face. She may someday write a book about her mission experiences, which should include all her letters, while serving others for eighteen months. Virginia is so full of energy and emotion. Her letters are lively and enjoyable. I am thankful now that I didn't give up on trying to overcome my lack of parenting skills and learning to parent her. There are so many things I would want to do differently, especially never losing my temper, composure and yelling at her. Yelling at someone because you are frustrated or angry is never productive. When I allowed her to push me too far, it usually led to me losing control and spanking her in anger. I hope that the openness of my troubles and mistakes will help other parents seek help if they struggle with the same problems. Please, parents, get help for yourself and family members, including the child that is manipulative or intense.

Chapter Four
She is a Joy to Others

Memories from Aunt Becky 2016

Virginia was just a toddler when her family left Utah and moved to Missouri. So I haven't known her as well as her older brother and sister. We did visit her family in Missouri, and they visited us as often as they could over the years. My most memorable time with Virginia was one summer's evening in the Bradley home. We were all inside the family kitchen. Virginia was out on the deck and entertaining us at the glass slider. She would put her open mouth on the window and blow. Our laughter fed her enthusiasm. The harder she blew, the larger her mouth appeared, and the louder we rollicked. It seemed like the show went on for hours. The reason I remember that evening was the intensity and the length of her show. Others tried to mimic Virginia's display once or twice and we all had a good laugh at everyone's attempt. However, Virginia continued to entertain with innumerable variations long after all others were done.

As Virginia grew, I took a special interest in her ability to sing. When she was in her early teens, she wrote a song and sent me a recording. I felt then that her emotional maturity was well beyond her years and her peers. Her first semester at college, she made the cuts to perform at a freshman talent show the first week of school. The reaction from the crowd at the performance verified that I am not the only one who appreciates her talent.—Rebecca Bracken

Thoughts from Grandma Joyce Bracken

Virginia came to see me a few months before she left on her mission before Christmas of 2015. She sang for me at the care center where I live in Nephi, Utah. I loved to show off my grandchildren to the other residents in the assisted living facility. I especially loved to have them show off their musical talents. And Virginia truly has talent.

A Memory of Debbie Mosteller

This was shared with me May 27, 2017. Debbie is my older sister and was living in Nephi, Utah at the time this took place.

This memory about Virginia took place when she was under eight years old. Debbie's family came to visit us in West Plains, Missouri. Debbie knew that I really could use a respite care provider because I was so exhausted from the constant tantrums and battles. She volunteered to take Virginia home to Utah with her for a week and then I would bring her home after I arrived one week later. I already had planned on a trip to Utah that particular summer anyway so sending Virginia out one week to ten days before we arrived was great. Debbie said that Virginia behaved wonderfully because she was in the honeymoon phase and so she wasn't a problem at all.

When I arrived in Utah, Virginia seemed happy to see me but not overjoyed. Debbie noticed that as soon as I arrived Virginia's behavior declined. She became upset about something and disappeared outside. I called for her and searched everywhere around the house, or so I thought. I climbed down into the creek bed calling and searching for her. This creek bed is usually dry and was at this time. It is just one hundred yards from my parents' home where I was staying with our children. My brother-in-law, sister and I looked for her for over an hour and it was getting dark. I was beginning to get worried because of the dry creek bed and all the many places she could have gone. Someone finally discov-

*ered her hiding in the old apple tree high up enough
so that we couldn't see her amongst the leaves, but she
could see us the entire time. I am sure that I was very
frustrated with her, but I was also glad that she was all
right.*

Carolyn Turner's Perspective

This next letter is from a friend of our family whom we
became acquainted with when Virginia was nine going on
ten. Her name is Carolyn Turner. We attended church with
Carolyn for nine years while we lived in Taos, Missouri.
She was Virginia's Young Women leader/pastor at church.
Carolyn was also Virginia's seminary teacher when she
was fifteen years old. Seminary is an early morning religion class that youth in our church attend during their high
school years. They usually meet at 5:30 or 6:00 a.m. for
fifty minutes! It is quite a sacrifice to get up so early before
school to attend a class five days a week the entire school
year. Most parents drive their child or children to this early
religion class until the student is old enough to drive there
on their own.

I was the seminary teacher for our little congregation for
six years. I taught our two older children throughout their
high school years and taught Virginia during her freshman
year. She was my most challenging student. Many times, if
she disagreed with a concept or principle, she would loudly
and boldly give her opinion. I had a hard time handling those

situations. Then I discovered that if I asked one of my other students to give their opinion about the principle that I had just explained, Virginia would not become as combative. During this religious class time, the students sang a hymn, read from the scriptures and discovered the doctrines of Jesus Christ. Carolyn taught Virginia in seminary for half of her sophomore year, and was Virginia's youth leader/pastor at the church we attended in Linn, Missouri for more than two years. Virginia's third seminary teacher was a man and she didn't like his style quite as well as she had Carolyn's. She would often complain about how the doctrine wasn't taught in his class, yet she was still learning and continued to attend. Her male seminary teacher really was fantastic; she just didn't like his technique. She would get up at five a.m. each morning and drive herself to seminary. This was a relief for me because I had been driving her to seminary for almost two years by that time.

A Letter from Carolyn Turner

I first met Virginia when she was about nine years old. She was outgoing, very vocal and demanded your attention, which can be usual behavior of that age. But, as time went on, I began to see that she craved attention and was very competitive. Whether in class or play she was eager to be the first and the best. Winning was important! Worth arguing over if she wasn't the winner.

After a few years, our families had the opportunity to interact more often and I became aware that there was a power struggle between Virginia and her mother. Virginia was often angry and vocal with her mother.

One evening, my husband and Mark (Virginia's father) were at a church meeting, when my husband called to say they would be late in returning because Mark had received an urgent call from home. During one of these power struggles, MaryAnn had restrained Virginia and was afraid she had broken Virginia's leg. Turned out there were no broken bones, just feelings.

On another occasion, Virginia and her father had words in the hallway of our church building and Virginia stormed out. Mark gave an apologetic glance and followed her outside. I do not know what started this or the previous occasion.

As Virginia grew, she seemed to learn how to better control herself. I could tell when she was upset but there were few outbursts. She seemed happy on the surface but often there was an underlying sadness. She did not often share details but did share that she often felt alone.

My favorite memory of Virginia is when she was about 13 years old. We spent most of a week together at a girls' summer camp. She was asked to share a tent with a girl a year younger. Virginia took her under her wing, showed her how to accomplish the tasks of camp and how to enjoy it. On the first night, everyone was tired and this younger girl was already homesick, when I heard Virginia's beautiful voice singing to comfort her.

Although still competitive, she showed a tender and compassionate side of herself as she helped her team, including this younger girl, to problem solve and compete in team activities. This tenderness and compassion continued after camp.

These young women were involved in two different church activities for the next year. Always eager to participate, I noticed that Virginia was not only willing to let others but encouraged them to do so.

She had grown so much in the years I knew her from a pretty self-absorbed little girl to a bright, enthusiastic, and compassionate young woman.

I love you, Virginia!!
Carolyn Turner

After reading this letter, I remembered the incident when Carolyn's husband came over to help Mark give Virginia a priesthood blessing. I mentioned it earlier in this story. I had forgotten that I was scared and thought Virginia's leg was broken or something else serious because she had twisted and turned so violently during the restraining time. And then she screamed that her leg was hurt. I indeed thought her leg was broken but, just as Carolyn said, of course her leg wasn't broken. Virginia was just putting on an act to get me to let her go.

Carolyn mentioned how she taught Virginia at church and attended Young Women's church camp with her one summer. I too had served as a volunteer for our church in the youth program. I had attended church camp with Virginia the previous year to the one Carolyn mentioned. The year I attended camp with Virginia, she was twelve and was pretty nervous about camping in her tent without me. I was staying in the lodge because I was one of the camp's cooks for the entire week. I recall Virginia sheepishly admitting she was a little scared about camping with all the other girls from the seven different congregations. I assured her that if she needed anything I was not too far away. After her first night in her tent, I was eager to find out how she had survived the night. It was her first time sleeping outdoors without our family. Virginia came and found me in the kitchen the next morning and hugged me. She told me how much she loved me. It was not unusual for her to hug me and tell me she loved me in public. She was much more comfortable in showing her affection in public than her other siblings were at her age. I asked her how she was doing and she smiled and said, "I am having a great time!" I was relieved that she had settled in so well.

I believe the greatest joy during her week at camp was spending so much time outside. While Virginia was at camp, she reached out to others during the week to encourage them when they were nervous or afraid. I found great satisfaction and joy observing her compassion for others, even though she herself had been feeling anxious. She didn't like to see others treated unkindly or unfairly. She was a champion of the underdog. She would become a fierce protector of anyone she felt was receiving unkind treatment.

Another interesting thing that Carolyn wrote in her letter was that Virginia often had this underlying sadness. I do not know if there was something that caused it or whether it was something she always struggled with. Earlier in my story, I wrote about the day when she was six or seven and she stood outside looking up into the heavens and asked God to take her home. Could this have been the depression the psychiatrist felt that she had? I do not know.

The following letter was written by one of my best friends, Malisa Cazier. She has known our family since Virginia was four years old. She has always been amazing with disciplining her children and never seemed to lose her cool. I learned a great deal from her. Malisa is wise beyond her years, and is much younger than me.

Malisa Cazier

*I met MaryAnn and her family through our mutual
church attendance. I was the young mother of five children, she a more experienced mother of four. I was in
awe of how well she did everything. MaryAnn seemed
to embody the spirit of Motherhood. She homeschooled
her children, kept an immaculate home, made bread
from scratch, had a beautiful meticulous garden, as
well as the wherewithal to devote time and energy to
physical and spiritual exercise. Her kids were well
versed and articulate. They followed their mother's
example of hard work and family. Mark (MaryAnn's
husband) is a likable guy with the ability to draw even
the most reserved into friendly conversation. He shares
her passion for work and family.*

*Mark was in the Air Force Reserves and called to
some greater activity after 9/11. Mark left to train
while MaryAnn stayed on the farm to continue caring
for their kids. Mark's absence was unavoidable but,
nonetheless, put a strain on the family. It was during
this time I began to have more interaction with her and
the kids. We talked several times a week on the phone
and at our kids' activities.*

*Virginia is a beautiful young woman; however, as a
child, she was captivating. She had beautiful auburn*

hair; her eyes were bright, eager and a little mischievous. Virginia's lips were so tiny and capable of such angelic music as well as sounds of significant anguish and hostility.

I remember a day in late spring when MaryAnn called and told me Virginia was having one of her fits. I knew of their trials with this behavior. Although I was naïve about the situation, I offered to come and help if I could. When I arrived, all other children were calm, the home in order. In fact, I may have never known anything was amiss if I hadn't heard Virginia's frustrated yells coming from her bedroom. She was screaming at the top of her angry voice, "I hate you! I hate this family! You don't love me! You are so mean!! E-V-E-R-Y-O-N-E is SO MEAN!"

I remember knocking on the door and just after my knock hearing crashing hit the wall next to the door. She was throwing the contents of her room at the door. She yelled, "I won't stop!" I must admit I was shocked at just how upset she was, and how unprepared I was to handle it. "Virginia," I said her name quiet but stern and pushed open the door. She stood there mid-throw, with a jewelry box in her hand ready to launch at the first sight of her mom. Her face was hot and angry with sweat and tears.

I walked over to her and took the box from her hand without any resistance. It was almost like my presence had snapped her out of some terrible rage. As I placed the box on her dresser, she crumpled to the ground, exhausted. I picked her tiny body up and held her on my lap. As we sat, her breathing slowed and she began to whimper. In less than four minutes, she was asleep. I sat there looking at her room; it was like a tiny tornado had touched down in there. She had taken pictures she had drawn of her happy loving family and torn them, pulled the neatly made covers off her bed and thrown them to the ground, as well as emptying the contents of her dresser onto the floor.

After ensuring she was asleep, I placed her in bed and went to find MaryAnn. She stood next to her bed folding clothes. I told her Ginny was asleep. MaryAnn apologized for having me come over. She looked exhausted.

I was happy to support my friend, but wondered aloud, "Why didn't you just spank her and put her in time out?"

MaryAnn looked up from folding and said, "The last time I did that... I bruised her."

My heart wept as I saw the humility and frustration

on her face. I walked over and hugged her and, as we embraced, I said, "Recognizing something is wrong is the first step to setting it right."

In that moment, my friend felt she had failed. In that same moment I felt like she was a success. She was able to admit something that mothers and women don't talk about, then took it a step further and acted on it.

Malisa Cazier

I do know this; we are all on this earth away from our Heavenly parents. Our time here is just a small blip in eternity. Most people feel sad when they first leave home, especially if that home was a loving and safe place to be. We believe our Heavenly home was a loving and safe place to which we will one day return. I know Virginia is a very spiritual person who has a wonderful connection to our Heavenly Father (God). My explanation for her underlying sadness, as Carolyn described it, varies at different stages of her life. As a very young child, I believe Virginia did feel a longing for her home in Heaven that she left to come to earth. The sadness she felt at other times in her life I would assume had to do with the constant turmoil she experienced with me as she tried to assert her independence at a very young age. I was a mother who expected a lot from my children. As I look back now, I am sure most of the time I expected too much of my children for certain things. I didn't really have a mature grasp on the concept of agency, or free will. Thus I believe that I didn't give her enough agency at times when I should have, but hindsight is 20/20.

Virginia was very competitive as are both of us (her parents.) Her father Mark is much more competitive than I am. When all our children were young and we played games together, Mark could not stand to lose. He would almost never let the children win at card games or other types of games and he admits it. I tried to encourage him when our children were young to let them win once in a while to build their confidence. He sometimes actually refused to let them win because he wanted to win himself!

Virginia graduated from high school one year ahead of her peers. She again was following in her older siblings' footsteps and attended BYU-Idaho where Janessa and John-Michael were both attending college. She lived with Janessa her first semester. This gave me comfort because I knew her sister and brother would look out for her and encourage her to obey the rules and stay out of trouble. She did very well academically. She stayed out past curfew a few times, after which her older siblings were able to teach her some valuable lessons about rules and safety.

Janessa told me the whole story about her concern for Virginia. She had been so worried about what might have happened to Virginia when she came home late one night. I thought to myself, "How grateful I am that Janessa is there." I was thankful that I didn't know about the incident until later. I would have worried about Virginia too much. Both Janessa and John-Michael served missions for our church and Virginia chose to serve one also. Janessa served in Oslo, Norway and John-Michael served in McAllen, Texas. Virginia received her mission call while she was attending college. Young adults can serve full-time missions—two years for young men and eighteen months for young women. Young men can serve when they turn eighteen and young women when they are nineteen.

A mission is voluntary and the application process can take several months. The applicant must be healthy physically and emotionally. Virginia had to receive a medical and dental exam. The application also requires ecclesiastical interviews with the applicants' bishop/pastor of their congregation. After all the paperwork, medical exams and myriad of interviews are complete, the applicants send their application to Salt Lake City, Utah, USA. Their application is reviewed by church authorities who are Apostles of The Church of Jesus Christ of Latter Day Saints. These apostles then prayerfully assign each young man or young woman to an area almost anywhere in the world. Some young people go to foreign-speaking missions as did Virginia's siblings. Virginia was called to serve in the Las Vegas, English-speaking mission, so she didn't have to learn a new language.

It was during Virginia's third semester at BYU-I that she received her mission call to the Nevada, Las Vegas

Mission. I had no idea how hard it would be for her and that she would want to give up and come home. I have an older brother who served a mission for our church over forty years ago. That particular brother went on to earn his PhD from a prestigious university several years later. Our oldest daughter Janessa told me that one of the hardest things she ever did was serve her mission to Norway. I know Virginia has the same capabilities to become whatever she puts her mind to.

The following is a short synopsis of a day in the mission field where Virginia served.

- 6:30 arise

- Between 6:30 and 10am exercise for 30 minutes, breakfast, get ready for the day, planning for the day 30 minutes, and personal study for 60 minutes.

- 10am to 9pm Proselyte (meaning go to set appointments with people who want to learn). Talk to everyone you see about the gospel and invite them to learn more. Knock on doors. Walk or drive to different locations and try to contact people who have talked to missionaries before talking to everyone.

- Lunch for 30 minutes.

- Companionship study 60 minutes, and dinner usually with members 60 minutes.

- 9pm go home write in journal and prepare for bed.
- 10:30 lights out.

Missionaries' work is hard and their days are exhausting. I remember when Virginia was seventeen, she decided to serve a mini-mission in Missouri with the full-time sister missionaries who were serving in St Louis at the time. This program is set up by the youth pastors who are in charge of 6-9 congregations of youth. The youth sign up to go out with missionaries and they have to be between sixteen and eighteen years old to qualify for this activity/service. I dropped Virginia off at the sisters' apartment on a Monday or Tuesday and she lived with the sister missionaries for three days and did everything they did. When I picked her up three days later, she was so exhausted that she came home and slept for two or three hours.

After she awoke, she exclaimed, "I don't think I want to serve a mission. You work so hard and it is exhausting!" I just chuckled to myself and hoped she would change her mind. She did, and I know she will never regret the choice she made to serve our God and the people of the Nevada, Las Vegas Mission for eighteen months.

Here is an excerpt from a letter to Mark and I (Mom) written by Virginia's mission president while she served in the Las Vegas area and Arizona for eighteen months. On this date, she had served in Las Vegas a few days shy of eleven months.

A Letter from Virginia's Mission President, January 26, 2017

RE: Virginia Joyce Bradley
New Leadership Assignment

Dear Brother and Sister Bradley,

It is an honor to serve with your wonderful daughter here in the Nevada Las Vegas Mission and I am pleased to announce that she has been assigned to serve as a Sister Training Leader. This is an important leadership position here in our mission that will allow her to share her amazing missionary skills with other missionaries-to-be as a role model and to provide important leadership to members of her zone.

Sister Bradley is an amazing missionary—truly worthy in every aspect to be the Savior's representative here in the Nevada Las Vegas Mission as he "Hastens the Work of Salvation." May I extend my appreciation to you for raising such a wonderful daughter of God and sharing her with us during this most important time in the history of mankind.—signed by her Mission President

This letter from Virginia's mission president showed the positive nature Virginia had been able to develop while she was under stress. Her mission president could see that her growth had come after great trials. She obviously learned how to become a good leader because she was given this responsibility. Her responsibility as a Sister Training Leader (STL) meant that she was in charge of several other companionships (groups of two) of other young adult women her age. She was in charge of making sure they received weekly encouragement and helped their companionships resolve conflicts if need be. She and her personal companion would call these companionships at least twice a week to make sure everything was going well with their work and their relationships with each other. If these companionships were not getting along with each other, their missionary work suffered. Virginia learned how to give positive advice and show compassion.

Here's an email sent to me from a woman/sister in Virginia's last area of her missionary service, Kingman, Arizona.

A Letter from Sister Anita Anderson

Dear Sister (MaryAnn Bradley),

I wanted to share with you this marvelous moment that I was honored to share with your daughter this evening at a new member baptism. I'm sure you may have heard of the beautiful evening that was had at the Baptism of George (name changed). But my thoughts are directed

*more toward the integrity and strength that I have been
a witness to while working with your daughter in the
mission field. I have personally been blessed by the
testimony that lies within your daughter's heart, and
her testimony that she so boldly shares with the children of God over in this small part of His Great Earth.
I have been strengthened by the spiritual guidance your
daughter abides by in honoring her calling.*

*I was a missionary once, over 25 years ago, in Jack-
son, Mississippi. I have been given the blessing of
re-experiencing missionary blessings that only come
thru serving with the sister missionaries. I'm so thankful for your desire to support your daughter on her
mission. I have been the recipient of God's goodness
and grace and the Holy Ghost's guidance directly
relating to your daughter's hard work and commitment
to her calling as a servant of the Lord. I have loved to
see my own testimony bloom while I have been serving
with your daughter.*

*Thank you again for your support of your beautiful
and talented daughter! My home is always open to
anything she may need. I hope she knows that and will
remember to call anytime. I'm a better person because
of her.*

Many thanks...

Sister Anita Anderson

The previous email/letter I received at 9:45 p.m. May 29, 2017. As I read the letter from Sister Anita Anderson, I was filled with so much joy and happiness. I am thrilled once again to hear from other people who have met Virginia and have felt her strong force for good in the world. Anita gave me permission to use her name.

A few years before Virginia served her mission, she underwent training to become a manager in one of her previous jobs. Virginia worked a few miles from our house at a local fast food restaurant. She excelled because of her vivacious personality and grit. The work environment was less than ideal. She worked mostly with adults and a few youth who constantly used inappropriate language and talked about things that were not conducive to an enjoyable working environment. Nonetheless, she moved up the chain to be a line manager.

One of Virginia's stressful days at work, the restaurant's manager took her aside. He told her that she was a great manager, but she needed to learn how to become a leader. At first, this constructive criticism annoyed her and caused her agitation. She came home ranting about how she felt he had gotten after her. His reprimand obviously hurt her feelings, especially when he told her she wasn't a leader. In spite of her hurt pride, she took his advice to heart. Virginia respected that particular manager and after some time she implemented his counsel. She worked on her behavior and responses to her co-workers. Later on, she was interviewed by a manager higher up on the food chain and received many compliments for her work ethic and leadership qualities. I am sure this particular work experience helped her to later become a great STL while she was serving as a missionary in the Las Vegas and Arizona areas for eighteen months.

After I read the letter from Virginia's mission president, I believed that Virginia was on yet another path of growth and great leadership development skills. She definitely learned how to become a leader, not just a manager. I will share one last excerpt from one of Virginia's mission letters. This particular letter jumped out at me as I reread many of her past emails. This email is dated August 2016. The following is just a small portion from that letter:

I am so privileged to be able to meet so many people! And for 18 months, such a short time, completely focus on others and help them come closer to their Savior. It is both the best thing ever and the hardest thing ever. We experience so much joy and face so much opposition. Sister H shared a poem with me that I feel perfectly describes how I feel about my mission... The Highs and Lows of a Mission:

"A mission is a strange experience
It is a trial and a test.
A mission throws at you the worst
Yet, teaches you the best.
I've never been so happy,
I've never been so depressed.
I've never felt so forsaken,
I've never felt so blessed.
I've never been so confused,
Things have never been so clear.
I've never felt my Heavenly Father so distant,
He's never been so near.
I've never been so discouraged,
I've never been so full of hope.
I feel I could go on for forever,
I think I've come to the end of my rope.
I've never had it quite so easy,
I've never had it quite so tough.
Things have never been so smooth,
Things have never been so rough.
I've never traveled through more valleys,
I've never ascended more peaks.
I've never met so many nice people.
I've never met so many freaks!
I've never had so many ups,
I've never had so many downs.
I've never worn so many smiles,

I've never had so many frowns.
I've never been so lonely,
I've never had so many friends.
BOY, I hope this is over soon,
GOSH, I hope this never ends.
So, yeah, if you ever think missionaries are bi-polar,
they're not; they're just missionaries."

I want all of you to know that this gospel, this church,
truly is Christ's. I know that the Book of Mormon is the
word of God and that Thomas S. Monson is His proph-
et today. I know that because I feel light and warmth
and peace every time I read their words. Do I fully
understand the why behind everything? No. But I have
faith that one day I will. All I know is that this gospel
has given me and my family more happiness and peace
than anything else ever has or could. Is it easy? No.
Of course not. But nothing that is worth anything is. I
encourage you to find out for yourself if what I say is
true. Go on! Ask God. He knows :)
All my love!
Sister Bradley

I got such a kick out of this line in her email, "So, yeah,
if you ever think missionaries are bi-polar, they're not;
they're just missionaries."

Virginia served valiantly, even when her emotions
seemed to engulf her. She took time out for herself to cry,

eat chocolate, and just talk to people so she could keep going. All of us have to take time for ourselves to reflect, have our feelings validated and sometimes just eat some comfort food. Serving a full-time mission is exhausting physically and emotionally. I am so proud of her for sticking through to the end. There were many times that she wanted to quit and just give up, but she didn't.

Not everyone who raises a Spirited/High Sensory child may feel like their child will ever reach a time when they are influencing others for good. Nor will every set of parents that have a child or children with these behavior patterns struggle with raising their children. I experienced so many days of self-loathing and complete discouragement. There was only one day when I asked God why he had given me this tough assignment. I sat by my bedroom window and sobbed uncontrollably, telling God I didn't like her and I didn't know what to do about it. I know that I, too, am an intense personality and because of that Virginia and I butted heads all the time. I am so thankful that I eventually met people and counselors that were able to help me see her as a precious daughter and how I needed to parent her with her unique behaviors.

My hope and prayer is that when you read about raising Virginia and our experiences, including all the mistakes we made as parents, you will feel encouraged. There is hope for anyone to change and overcome challenges or learn how to use those challenges and create something productive. I have gained so much compassion and respect for parents who have raised or are raising spirited/intense/high sensory children. We must never judge other parents for their parenting techniques or lack thereof. We each have unique children. Each child is a gift and can be taught to become amazing adults. With the help of so many friends, counselors, and God, Virginia has become and continues to become an amazing adult.

She has grown exponentially beyond what I had imagined over the course of her mission. She has touched so many lives during the eighteen months that she spent in the Nevada and Arizona areas of her mission. I know Virginia will continue to touch lives for the rest of her life. My prayer is that she will always remain close to God, our Heavenly Father, so that her influence will be a force for light and truth wherever she goes.

www.ingramcontent.com/pod-product-compliance
Lightning Source LLC
Chambersburg PA
CBHW061731020426
42331CB00006B/1199